W9-BNP-706

thefacts

Schizophrenia

➔ also available in the**facts** series

Eating disorders: the**facts**
FIFTH EDITION
Abraham

Sexually transmitted infections:
the**facts**
THIRD EDITION
Barlow

Thyroid disease: the**facts**
FOURTH EDITION
Vanderpump and Tunbridge

Living with a long-term illness:
the**facts**
Campling

Prenatal tests: the**facts**
DeCrespigny

Obsessive-compulsive disorder:
the**facts**
THIRD EDITION
De Silva

The pill and other forms of
hormonal contraception: the**facts**
SIXTH EDITION
Guillebaud

Myotonic dystrophy: the**facts**
Harper

Ankylosing spondylitis: the**facts**
Khan

Prostate cancer: the**facts**
Mason

Multiple sclerosis: the**facts**
FOURTH EDITION
Matthews

Essential tremor: the**facts**
Plumb

Panic disorder: the**facts**
SECOND EDITION
Rachman

Tourette syndrome: the**facts**
Robertson

Adhd: the**facts**
Selikowitz

Dyslexia and other learning
difficulties: the**facts**
SECOND EDITION
Selikowitz

Schizophrenia: the**facts**
THIRD EDITION
Tsuang

Depression: the**facts**
Wassermann

Polycystic ovary syndrome:
the**facts**
Elsheikh and Murphy

Autism and Asperger syndrome:
the**facts**
Baron-Cohen

Motor neuron disease: the**facts**
Talbot and Marsden

Lupus: the**facts**
SECOND EDITION
Isenberg and Manzi

Muscular Dystrophy: the**facts**
THIRD EDITION
Emery

Osteoarthritis: the**facts**
Arden, Arden, and Hunter

Cosmetic surgery: the**facts**
Waterhouse

the**facts**

Schizophrenia

THIRD EDITION

MING T. TSUANG

Behavioral Genomics Endowed Chair and University Professor,
University of California: Distinguished Professor
of Psychiatry and Director, Center for Behavioral Genomics,
Department of Psychiatry, University of California,
San Diego, La Jolla, California
USA

STEPHEN V. FARAONE

Director, Medical Genetics Research
Professor of Psychiatry and of Neuroscience and Physiology
Director, Child and Adolescent Psychiatry Research
SUNY Upstate Medical University
Syracuse, New York
USA

STEPHEN J. GLATT

Director, Psychiatric Genetic Epidemiology and Neurobiology
Laboratory (PsychGENe Lab)
Assistant Professor, Department of Psychiatry and Behavioral Sciences
Assistant Professor, Department of Neuroscience and Physiology
Associate Director, Medical Genetics Research Center (MGRC)
SUNY Upstate Medical University
Syracuse, New York
USA

OXFORD
UNIVERSITY PRESS

OXFORD
UNIVERSITY PRESS

Great Clarendon Street, Oxford OX2 6DP

Oxford University Press is a department of the University of Oxford.
It furthers the University's objective of excellence in research, scholarship,
and education by publishing worldwide in

Oxford New York

Auckland Cape Town Dar es Salaam Hong Kong Karachi
Kuala Lumpur Madrid Melbourne Mexico City Nairobi
New Delhi Shanghai Taipei Toronto

With offices in

Argentina Austria Brazil Chile Czech Republic France Greece
Guatemala Hungary Italy Japan Poland Portugal Singapore
South Korea Switzerland Thailand Turkey Ukraine Vietnam

Oxford is a registered trade mark of Oxford University Press
in the UK and in certain other countries

Published in the United States
by Oxford University Press Inc., New York

© Oxford University Press, 2011

The moral rights of the authors have been asserted
Database right Oxford University Press (maker)

First edition published 1982
Second edition published 1997

All rights reserved. No part of this publication may be reproduced,
stored in a retrieval system, or transmitted, in any form or by any means,
without the prior permission in writing of Oxford University Press,
or as expressly permitted by law, or under terms agreed with the appropriate
reprographics rights organization. Enquiries concerning reproduction
outside the scope of the above should be sent to the Rights Department,
Oxford University Press, at the address above

You must not circulate this book in any other binding or cover
and you must impose this same condition on any acquirer

British Library Cataloguing in Publication Data

Data available

Library of Congress Cataloguing in Publication Data

Data available

Typeset in Plantin
by Glyph International, Bangalore, India
Printed in Great Britain
on acid-free paper by
Clays Ltd, St Ives plc

ISBN 978-0-19-960091-5

10 9 8 7 6 5 4 3 2 1

While every effort has been to ensure that the contents of this book are as complete, accurate
and up-to-date as possible at the date of writing, Oxford University Press is not able to give
any guarantee or assurance that such is the case. Readers are urged to take appropriately
qualified medical advice in all cases. The information in this book is intended to be useful to
the general reader, but should not be used as a means of self-diagnosis or for the prescription of
medication. The authors and the publishers do not accept responsibility or legal liability for any
errors in the text or for the misuse or misapplication of material in this book.

Acknowledgements

The authors would like to thank Cheryl Roe and Sean Bialosuknia for editorial assistance and background research. Preparation of this book was supported in part by grants R01MH065562, R01MH071912, and R21MH075027 from the National Institute of Mental Health, and the Lieber Prize for Schizophrenia Research from NARSAD, the Brain and Behavior Research Fund, awarded to Dr. Tsuang, as well as grants R01MH085521 and P50MH081755-0003 from the National Institute of Mental Health, and a Katowitz/Radin Young Investigator Award and the Sidney R. Baer, Jr. Prize for Schizophrenia Research from NARSAD, the Brain and Behavior Research Fund, awarded to Dr. Glatt.

Preface

The primary purpose of this book is to provide the lay reader with an introduction to the current state of scientific knowledge regarding the brain disorder known as schizophrenia. Without in any way seeking to exclude the professional reader trained in psychiatry or any other branch of medicine or other mental health professionals, we are primarily concerned with helping persons affected with schizophrenia, their relatives, close friends, caregivers, and other acquaintances understand the condition more fully.

To accomplish this aim, we must necessarily employ some specialist terms from the vocabulary of mental health. In doing so, however, we have attempted to adhere to two guiding principles: technical terms will always be clearly defined, and we shall endeavor to steer clear of the use of jargon and 'buzz words' within the discipline of mental health—that is the kind of semi-slang words that professionals in any field use among themselves as a convenient shorthand for more cumbersome terms with meanings that are mutually understood. One example of this, which has changed since the last edition of this book, is our attempt to describe the facts as they pertain to 'individuals with schizophrenia', rather than 'schizophrenics', as we understand these individuals now as suffering from and living with a brain disorder rather than being defined by it.

Concerning references to research in the book, we have kept these to a minimum, partly for reasons of space, but more so to promote easy reading and facilitate readers' processing of 'the facts' as we see them. This is not an academic text and we do not feel it would assist the reader materially to know the source, date, and author of every study used in the book. Naturally, research projects of major importance to the study of schizophrenia—and the investigators who lead them—are identified and documented more fully. Conversely, you may notice that some of the latest and most novel results reported in the scientific literature may not be described fully in the book. Although in many cases we are aware of these studies and are following such developments closely, we have restricted our discussion to topics about which enough is known and enough has been reliably reproduced that they deserve mention in a book subtitled 'the facts'.

Ming T. Tsuang, La Jolla, California
Stephen V. Faraone and Stephen J. Glatt, Syracuse,
New York
2011

Contents

1

What is schizophrenia?

> ## ➔ Key points
>
> ◆ Schizophrenia is a disabling disease in which those affected experience altered thoughts, perceptions, emotions, and behaviours.
>
> ◆ Rather than a unitary disorder, schizophrenia is now believed to comprise a 'spectrum' of related conditions with variable severity, course, and outcome.

Schizophrenia is a mental illness that has major consequences for affected individuals, their families, and society. Affected individuals may show a wide range of disruptions in their ability to see, hear, and otherwise process information from the world around them. They may also experience disruptions in their normal thought processes, as well as their emotions and their behaviours. For many individuals with schizophrenia, the disturbance of such basic aspects of life can be crippling, resulting in a lifetime of disability, periodic hospitalizations, and a failure of family and social relationships. These relationships are often disrupted as a direct consequence of the affected individual's withdrawal and inability to communicate which may alternate with bouts of disruptive behaviour. The alienation of the affected individual from the family easily can be exacerbated by the strain of caring for a mentally ill relative and the stigma of mental illness. Because the disorder is so severe, and because many people will be afflicted with the disorder at some time in their life, schizophrenia is now recognized as a major public health concern.

Schizophrenia is a tremendously complex disorder in both its **aetiology** (causes) and its presentation. Although the illness has been studied for over a century, much remains unknown about its origins, development, pathology and treatment; however, progress in unravelling these mysteries has accelerated in the last 40 years. Some of these advances come from improvements in methods used to study the disorder, such as brain-imaging technologies and molecular-genetic techniques. Another source of this enhanced understanding is the continual re-conceptualization and re-formulation of the schizophrenia diagnosis. Current approaches view schizophrenia as a point–or endpoint–on a continuum of abnormal psychological functioning rather than a discrete disease entity; this view has changed the way in which the remaining questions about the disease are approached.

The notion of a '**spectrum**' of schizophrenias, comprised of schizophrenia and a number of related–but generally milder–conditions, is not new. The concept was advanced by Eugen Bleuler, who foreshadowed current views in his 1911 work *Dementia Praecox*, or *The Group of Schizophrenias*. We now know that disorders such as schizoaffective disorder and schizotypal, paranoid, and schizoid personality disorders share some clinical features with schizophrenia, and may also share a causal basis. This knowledge has facilitated the search for common risk factors and treatments. The increasing breadth and depth of our understanding of schizophrenia as a discrete or distinct diagnosis has also had the reverse effect; i.e., with ever-increasing knowledge of the foundations of schizophrenia, inroads have been made into elucidating the specific pathologies and treatments of the other schizophrenia spectrum disorders by their analogy to schizophrenia-specific features.

2

What is not schizophrenia?

> ## ➲ Key points
>
> ◆ Despite the common misconception, schizophrenia is not to be confused
>   with ambivalence (being of two minds or two opinions on a matter),
>   or 'multiple-personality' or dissociative identity disorder.

The words 'schizophrenia' and 'schizophrenic' are commonly misused in our
daily conversation and in the popular news media. They mean different things
to different people: an attitude of mind, a description of a personality, or a
psychiatric illness. For example, someone unable to make up his mind or with
simultaneous feelings of hate and love for a particular person may be labeled
schizophrenic ('ambivalent' is the more appropriate term). In some cultures,
especially in the past, schizophrenia was seen as a sign of possession by an
evil spirit or, ironically, as an indicator of religious superiority. Persons with
schizophrenia were either punished or praised in accordance with the beliefs
of their culture.

Today, the most common misconception is that a person with schizophrenia
has a 'split' or multiple personality. This is decidedly not true. Unfortunately,
this sort of indiscriminate usage was once common in the fields of medicine,
psychology, and sociology. Indeed, several decades ago, any kind of 'nervous
breakdown' might have been called schizophrenic, and clinicians diagnosed
schizophrenia in people with widely varying degrees of madness, derange-
ment, depression, or personality problems. As you begin to learn about this
illness, please discard any preconceptions you may have picked up from casual

conversation or the popular press. As we will show, the correct use of the word 'schizophrenia' is as a diagnostic term used to define a specific mental condition according to well-specified and researched criteria. When we use this word precisely, it has very specific implications for the treatment of the condition, the course of the disorder, and our knowledge about its causes.

3

What are the symptoms of schizophrenia?

Key points

- Hallucinations of hearing voices, delusions of being controlled by others, emotional blunting, and lack of insight are examples of schizophrenia symptoms that occur regardless of culture or language.

- Positive symptoms of schizophrenia denote the production of abnormal phenomena. These include hallucinations and delusions.

- Negative symptoms denote lack of emotions and feeling, blunted affect, and loss of normal behaviours. These include affective blunting or flattening (inability to express emotions), alogia (poverty or disruption of speech), avolition (lack of will to interact with the world), anhedonia (the inability to experience pleasure), asociality (the preference for isolation), and catatonia, which is a group of four cognitive and motor symptoms.

- Negative symptoms are typically less easily identified and treated than positive symptoms. Compared to positive symptoms, they are less disruptive to others but cause considerable disability to patients.

One of the simplest ways to understand the clinical picture of schizophrenia is to divide it into two categories: positive and negative symptoms. **Positive symptoms** show up as behaviours not seen in the normal repertoire of human activities, whereas negative symptoms refer to important behaviours that are eliminated from the behavioural repertoire. Positive symptoms predominate during the 'active' phase of the illness, when an affected individual is most disturbed and disruptive. The active phase usually leads to the individual's hospitalization or referral for care because they typically will be doing or saying things that bother people around them. For example, a delusional patient might complain to her spouse that she is being followed by space aliens and demand that he help her find a way to stop them. Negative symptoms predominate during the '**prodromal**' and '**residual**' phases of the illness. The prodromal phase precedes the first active phase, and the residual phase follows the active phase.

Positive symptoms

This class of symptoms includes, most commonly, delusions, and auditory, visual, or other sensory hallucinations. Positive symptoms can be classified as **perceptual** (i.e., affecting perception, or the ability to become aware of some stimulus through the senses), **cognitive** (i.e., affecting thought processes), **emotional**, or **motoric**, depending on which area of behaviour is involved. Because these symptoms are so recognizable, even to the untrained eye, they constitute a large part of the lay person's general image of schizophrenia.

Auditory hallucinations are the most common perceptual abnormalities observed in schizophrenia. Many times, these hallucinations take the form of a voice, sometimes delivering a running commentary on the individual's thoughts or behaviours, and sometimes they take the form of several voices, each conversing with the other. Some patients with schizophrenia have **visual**, **olfactory** (i.e., affecting the sense of smell), or **gustatory** (i.e., affecting taste) **hallucinations**, but these are rare. **Somatic hallucinations** may also occur, in which the misperception is centered at or on the body's organs.

It is important here to differentiate between hallucinations, which are perceptions or experiences that occur in the absence of a stimulus, and **illusions**, which are perceptions occurring in response to ambiguous stimuli. For example, in response to questions about visual hallucinations, one of our patients said he had seen his dead mother one evening. Further questioning revealed that the patient had seen someone who resembled his mother, and this resemblance was accentuated in the dim light. Although this episode may be informative about the patient's reactions to his mother's death, it was an illusion, not a hallucination indicative of schizophrenia. Recurrent illusions may occur during the prodromal and residual phases of the illness. Visual hallucinations should also not be confused with the 'hypnagogic' imagery that many individuals experience before falling asleep.

Delusions are false beliefs that are not open to change by reason or experience even though the person is in a clear state of consciousness; these are the most common thought disruption observed in schizophrenia. Interestingly, the content of a delusion ordinarily relates to the affected individual's cultural context, while the source of the delusion is typically personal. In Franz Mesmer's day, individuals with schizophrenia spoke of being influenced by magnetism; 100 years ago, by electricity; and 40 years ago, by television. Now they may speak of being influenced by computers or the internet.

Despite the great variety of delusions exhibited by people with schizophrenia, many types of delusions may have a common theme. For example, individuals who experience **paranoid delusions** report that others are trying to harm them, either emotionally or physically. Like other delusions, these are easy to recognize because their components are clearly absurd (for example, a patient may complain that her mother is plotting with extraterrestrial creatures to prevent her from graduating from high school). In some cases, however, a paranoid belief may appear false because it is improbable, but may actually be grounded in fact. For example, one of our patients had a fear of being assaulted by Mafia thugs, which was shown to be non-delusional after careful assessment of his previous criminal activities.

Patients with **delusions of sin or guilt** believe they are being punished, or should be punished, for some misdeed. These delusions may relate to real events or to fictional ones, but even when the misdeed is real, the punishment conjured by the individual far outweighs the offence in severity (e.g., the patient feels condemned to remain in a closet for the rest of his life because he forgot to mow the lawn for his father). Paranoid and guilty delusions differ in that the paranoid individual believes the claimed persecution is undeserved, whereas the delusionally guilty individual believes the punishment is deserved. Since delusions of sin or guilt are often seen in mood disorders with psychotic features, affected individuals should be carefully evaluated for the signs of mood dysregulation seen in depression or bipolar disorder.

Delusions of jealousy convey the belief that a spouse or lover has been unfaithful, but such delusions are often difficult to evaluate. In the absence of bizarre components, the delusion can be evaluated by the affected individual's ability to integrate the relevant evidence for and against the delusion. When confronted with evidence contrary to the delusional belief, the truly delusional individual will ignore or rationalize such evidence and, as might be expected, even the most minute piece of evidence supporting the delusion is vigorously embraced and aggressively discussed.

Somatic delusions are often related to somatic hallucinations, in that the source of the delusion is the affected individual's own body. These delusions are generally bizarre and unsettling in nature, and typically convey a belief that the individual's body is being harmed or injured. For example, one patient believed his intestines were being devoured by a giant worm. Another was certain he would soon die because his body was rotting from the inside outward. These delusions can also occur in other psychiatric conditions, such as depression with psychotic features and delusional disorder, and so these disorders must be carefully differentiated from the delusions of schizophrenia. Somatic delusional disorders are rare and resemble other hypochondriacal disturbances in which concerns with and fear about physical health are prominent. The difference lies in the degree of conviction: for the delusional individual, the disease or change in appearance is real, usually bizarre, not grounded in reality, and not open to change.

Patients with **grandiose delusions** exaggerate their talents and accomplishments to an unrealistic or even bizarre level. An extreme example would be a patient who claimed to be 'king of the universe' because of his special relationship with God. In milder cases, the individual may claim to have extraordinary talents that are not substantiated (for example, a patient who claims to be a great mathematician although his alleged mathematical proofs are meaningless scrawls). Because grandiosity is also a common feature of mania and hypomania, such symptoms should be evaluated carefully to differentiate these conditions from the grandiose delusions of schizophrenia.

If the affected individual presents with false beliefs involving religious or spiritual themes, he may be suffering from a **religious delusion**. The delusional status of a religious belief may be obvious, as in the case of a patient who collected a roomful of grapefruits because she believed they contained the essence of God. However, the delusional status of religious beliefs may be more difficult to establish than that of other types of delusions since a religious belief is not considered delusional if it is consistent with the individual's cultural context. For example, many Jehovah's Witnesses believe in the imminent end of the world. Such a belief would not be delusional if expressed by a member of that sect, but it might be delusional if expressed by a non-religious person. Some individuals with schizophrenia may be attracted by unusual religious sects. If this is suspected, then the possibly delusional religious belief should be explored for either a history that precedes the patient's association with the sect or components that are absurd even in the context of the sect.

Other categories of delusions include the **bizarre delusions**, in which the content of the belief is illogical and can have no possible basis in fact, and **delusions of being controlled**, in which the affected individual believes that his mind or body is being controlled by an outside source at a level that exceeds mere persuasion or coercion. Other common delusions involve the belief that an individual's thoughts are being manipulated by an outside agency in any number of ways. One example of this type of delusion includes **thought broadcasting**, in which the affected individual believes his ideas are being spoken aloud so that others can hear them. Another example is **thought**

insertion, wherein the individual experiences ideas being inserted into his stream of consciousness by an outside source. The nature of these thoughts is typically unpleasant, and the 'inserted' thoughts may direct the individual to engage in abnormal behaviours. The opposite of thought insertion is **thought withdrawal** and, as its name suggests, this delusion is experienced by the individual as the active removal of thoughts from the stream of consciousness, and the loss of ideas is, again, typically attributed to an outside agency. This process often manifests as **blocking**, which is a sudden stop in the stream of speech.

The catalogue of delusions outlined above illustrates the staggering diversity of cognitive disruption commonly observed in people with schizophrenia. Clinicians use a set of criteria to assess the severity of a delusion along five dimensions: persistence, complexity, bizarreness, behavioural impact, and degree of doubt. The **persistence** of the delusion is measured both as the permanence of the belief and the frequency with which the delusion draws upon the affected individual's mental resources. Some patients report delusions that have affected them on a daily basis for months or even years, while others will report episodic delusions that come and go, and which last only several hours at a time.

The essence of a delusion's **complexity** is the extent to which the delusion forms an integrated idea or set of ideas. Sometimes, complexity is quite low, such as when an individual believes that he is the president of the United States but does not develop any elaborate themes or stories associated with his high office. A similar but very complex delusion is illustrated by the case of a patient who believed he was the president of the United States in disguise because of assassination threats by the KGB. He had chosen a job as a bank teller because it would allow him to control the money supply of the country, which was his ultimate source of power. Such a delusion might elaborate into greater levels of complexity and include friends, relatives, or even strangers who played some role in this unusual story.

Delusions can also vary in their levels of **bizarreness** or, alternatively, credibility. Some patients will voice bizarre delusions that have no credibility whatsoever. Other patients may express seemingly bizarre delusions that achieve some level of credibility when the patient's cultural context is considered. This situation often occurs when the patient comes from a deviant cultural context (for example, the criminal community or an unusual religious sect) and expresses beliefs consistent with that context. If a belief is possibly delusional, it is useful to allow the affected individual to discuss the implications of the belief and associated ideas. With further discussion, a culturally reasonable but unusual belief may blossom into a complex and bizarre delusional system.

A delusion's **behavioural impact** is gauged by its ability to inspire action on the part of the affected individual. At one extreme, a patient may only discuss a delusion when asked about it and may never perform any related actions. At the other extreme, a patient may constantly preach his delusional belief to strangers and take extreme, self-damaging actions based on it (e.g., the patient may burn his house down because he believes it is contaminated with evil spirits that are trying to kill him). Individuals also vary on the **degree of doubt** attached to delusions. Some patients believe their delusions with full conviction; others may have bizarre ideas that they think might be true with varying degrees of certainty.

While delusions are the most common thought disruptions seen in schizophrenia, these can be accompanied by another type of dysfunction called **markedly illogical thinking**. For example, an individual with schizophrenia might reason, 'The president of the United States is Protestant; I am Protestant; therefore I am the president of the United States'. An affected individual's reasoning may also be impaired by a **loosening of associations,** a process by which the individual connects seemingly unrelated concepts to each other. Thought and language usually have a high degree of sequential cohesiveness that emerges from the stringing together of ideas and/or images that are consensually related to one another. Obliquely related responses to questions are examples of **tangentiality**. In a normal conversation, for example, it is reasonable for a person to respond to another's description of a fishing vacation by describing his own vacation or asking questions about the other's vacation. An individual with schizophrenia might respond by talking about a tuna fish sandwich that he had the other day. For the individual with schizophrenia, the loose association between a fishing vacation and tuna fish sandwich is enough to justify the transition. Associations can become so idiosyncratic and remote that no connection at all is observed between different components of an affected individual's speech. In the extreme case, individuals with schizophrenia may speak **word salad**; that is, most of the words in any given sentence appear to have no syntactic or semantic connection to one another.

In addition to the many cognitive disruptions that are readily apparent in their speech and thought processes, people with schizophrenia also commonly exhibit signs of abnormal emotional regulation. This disruption of emotional functioning is usually observed in one of two forms: **inappropriate affect** or **excessive emotional excitement**. Inappropriate affect refers to giggling, self-absorbed smiling, or a mood that is incongruent or inconsistent with expressed ideas. For example, one patient may grin or chuckle while discussing the death of his brother whom he loved dearly. Another may continually grin or scowl in a bizarre fashion regardless of context. Excessive emotional excitement is often seen in agitated individuals, who may experience appropriate emotions but, because of delusional thinking or other factors, may express these emotions too intensely.

An extreme state of motor excitement seen in some individuals with schizophrenia also qualifies as a positive symptom of the disorder. This agitated state, termed **catatonic excitement**, consists of irregular episodes of uncontrolled and disorganized movement. The individual may gesticulate excessively, and be hyperactive, destructive, or violent. Motor dysfunction is also evidenced as repetitive, apparently meaningless movements known as **stereotypies**. People with schizophrenia also exhibit characteristic mannerisms, consisting of habitual movements that usually involve a single body part (grimaces, tics, moving lips soundlessly, fidgeting with fingers, hand wringing, or thigh rubbing).

Negative symptoms

The negative symptoms of schizophrenia are those in which an important or normally occurring aspect of an individual's behavioural repertoire has become deficient or absent. Just like positive symptoms, negative symptoms affect the cognitive, emotional, and behavioural aspects of one's life, but do so in the direction of decreased expressiveness and responsiveness. Negative symptoms may be more chronic and, in some ways, more devastating than positive symptoms; however, negative symptoms do not typically lead to hospitalization because, unlike positive symptoms, they usually do not negatively impact or otherwise impinge upon other people, and therefore do not bring the patient to the attention of legal or medical authorities. Negative symptoms are more difficult to define and, historically, have been more difficult to rate reliably, and to treat effectively.

There are several indices of cognitive disruption in schizophrenia; however, most of these index positive symptoms of the disorder. Some, however, do identify areas of cognitive insufficiency that are clearly negative symptoms. The most common are those that reflect diminished productivity of thought. **Poverty of speech** means that the individual says very little on his own initiative or in response to questions or situations that would normally evoke verbal responses. The extreme case is **mutism**, in which an individual does not speak at all even though he is physically capable of doing so. **Poverty of content of speech** is evident when the individual's verbal productivity is normal but the verbalization conveys very little information. **Increased latency of response** refers to a notable lag in the affected individual's responses to questions. Blocking occurs when the patient's stream of speech suddenly stops and he is incapable of continuing. This behaviour is often seen in conjunction with thought withdrawal.

The negative symptom of schizophrenia that is characterized by a reduction or absence of emotional responsiveness is called **flat, blunt,** or **restricted affect**. Restricted affect may be observed in the individual's lack of vocal inflections, paucity of expressive gestures, poor eye contact, decreased spontaneous movements, unchanging facial expression, or a non-responsive mood. Another commonly reported negative mood symptom of schizophrenia is **anhedonia,** or the inability to experience pleasure. Often, signs of anhedonia are readily reflected in the affected individual's lack of interest in recreation, friendships, sexuality, or any activity that he previously found enjoyable. Diminished emotional responsiveness is also seen in the individual's diminished ability to feel intimacy or closeness with others.

Catatonic stupor is a negative motor symptom of schizophrenia characterized by a paucity of movement and communication. Some patients may exhibit **waxy flexibility**, in which they passively allow others to manipulate their limbs into positions that are sometimes uncomfortable. **Posturing** (also known as **catalepsy**) refers to holding unusual or uncomfortable positions for long periods during a catatonic stupor. Catatonia in schizophrenia used to be fairly common, but is now quite rare. This change cannot be unambiguously ascribed to one factor, but some possibilities include changes in hospital admission practises, better treatment of the disorder before catatonia emerges, or changes in the social environment, such as the types of drugs (both prescribed and illicit) available for use.

A related negative symptom of schizophrenia is **negativism,** in which the patient exhibits strong resistance to any verbal or physical attempts to engage him. More common behavioural impairments are poor grooming and hygiene, inability to persist at tasks, and withdrawal from social activities. The systematic study of social behaviour in patients with schizophrenia has shown that the disorder results in a marked loss of the basic behavioural components necessary for effective social interaction.

4

How is schizophrenia diagnosed?

➔ Key points

- Many conditions cause symptoms similar to those of schizophrenia, so it is important that persons suspected of having schizophrenia get proper medical care including a differential diagnosis so that the clinicians treating the patient know how to best treat the patient's condition.

- Differential diagnoses are crucial in the treatment of patients with schizophrenia to rule out other conditions that could possibly cause the patient's condition, such as encephalitis, drug abuse, epilepsy, or well-defined brain diseases.

- Schizophrenia is not a mood disorder. Persons with mood disorders exhibit periods of mania and depression where they experience very high emotional states of euphoria, talkativeness, and high activity (mania), or very low emotional states of depression and feelings of worthlessness (depression).

- Delusions are one symptom type that both mood disorders and schizophrenia share, though they differ greatly between the two. In mania, the delusions held by the patient are often grandiose in nature, while delusions of worthlessness and guilt may be present in depression. In schizophrenia delusions are usually bizarre or paranoid.

- People who exhibit symptoms of schizophrenia as well as the aberrations of mood found in affective disorders may be categorized as having a schizoaffective disorder.

Although many theories abound regarding the causes of schizophrenia, none has yet to be validated. As such, the diagnosis of schizophrenia cannot currently be made based on the results of a diagnostic test or laboratory assessment, though we and others are working towards this. Instead, the modern diagnosis of schizophrenia is based on descriptive patterns of behaviour and psychopathology (including the symptoms described above) that can be reliably assessed.

Since 1980, the definitions of major mental illnesses have been catalogued in the form of the Diagnostic and Statistical Manual (**DSM**) of the American Psychiatric Association (in the United States) and the World Health Organization's International Classification of Diseases (**ICD**) in other countries. These definitions are updated occasionally to reflect advances in knowledge, or to reflect modern conceptualizations of the relatedness or distinctness of certain disorders as compared to others. From one edition to the next, some diagnoses are revised, some are added, and some vanish altogether, only to be replaced or subsumed under others.

The diagnostic criteria of schizophrenia as defined by the most recent version of the DSM (DSM-IV-TR) are aggregated into six sets, labeled A–F. Criterion A requires the presence, in some form, of the massive disruptions in cognition and/or perception that the clinician Emil Kraepelin identified as the core features of the disorder over a century ago. If the individual exhibits certain types of delusions, auditory hallucinations, thought disorder, catatonia, or negative symptoms, criterion A has been met.

Kraepelin's belief that schizophrenia is also characterized by a chronic and progressively worsening course is reflected in both criteria B and C. If a patient exhibits a clear indication of deterioration in social or occupational functioning and demonstrates continuous signs of the illness for at least 6 months, then these two criteria have been met.

The purpose of criterion D is to differentiate schizophrenia from full depressive or manic disorders with psychotic features in order to make sure that the diagnosis of schizophrenia represents a relatively homogeneous set of patients with common features. If a full depressive or manic syndrome were exhibited, the patient would not receive a diagnosis of schizophrenia unless the mood disturbance developed after the active phase of the schizophrenia syndrome or was brief in relation to it.

Criteria E and F require that the illness be not better accounted for by a general medical condition, substance use, or a pervasive developmental disorder. These exclusions are necessary because other conditions are known to mimic the signs and symptoms of schizophrenia.

When these diagnostic criteria are applied appropriately, the reliance on observable disturbances minimizes inferences or 'best guesses,' and improves the likelihood that two independent clinicians can diagnose the same individual with the same disorder. In this scheme, there is no room for speculation regarding potential causal factors. However, the process of formulating a diagnosis is not a rote exercise in tallying the number of criteria met; sound clinical judgement is still required. With structured criteria, clinical judgement enters into the evaluation of whether the symptoms within a specific, well-defined criterion are present or absent. Thus, the presence of structured diagnostic criteria in the DSM-IV-TR has not eliminated the need for clinical judgement; it has merely focused this judgement on the data-collection process of the diagnostic work. The presentation of these criteria in the DSM-IV-TR is quite clear, but the variety of clinical manifestations of this disorder can be very difficult to gauge accurately.

Subtypes of schizophrenia

Although Kraepelin originally characterized *dementia praecox* as a single disorder, he and his contemporaries also recognized that there were many different ways in which schizophrenia appears. Initially, Kraepelin made the distinction between hebephrenic, catatonic, and paranoid subtypes of schizophrenia, and the clinician Eugen Bleuler later added a subtype called simple schizophrenia. The use of the term 'schizophrenic disorders' instead of 'schizophrenia' to describe this illness in the DSM-IV-TR emphasizes this variety of clinical presentations, and the use of these subtypes in the DSM-IV-TR is also a testament to the observational acumen of these early psychopathologists. Five major subtypes of schizophrenia are now recognized: paranoid, disorganized, catatonic, undifferentiated, and residual.

The hallmark of **paranoid schizophrenia** is a preoccupation with one or several delusions or persistent auditory hallucinations. Paranoid delusions are usually persecutory or grandiose in nature, but other delusions can occur. Many times, the hallucinations experienced by the individual are related to the nature of his delusions. Along with these features, the individual may harbor a sense of unremitting suspicion and may appear tense, guarded, and reserved to the point of vagueness or even mutism. While delusions and/or hallucinations are almost universally seen in individuals with this subtype of schizophrenia, other clinical features, such as hostility, aggression, and even violence, may be present in varying degrees. Paranoid patients show only mild, if any, impairments on neuropsychological tests, and their long-term prognosis is typically better than that of individuals with other schizophrenia subtypes.

As its name suggests, **disorganized schizophrenia** is characterized by muddled or confused speech, disorganized behaviour, and flat or inappropriate affect.

The patient with disorganized schizophrenia may voice hypochondriacal complaints and express bizarre thoughts. Often these patients exhibit bizarre behaviours as well, and may suffer from severe social withdrawal. The patient may also have fragmentary delusions or hallucinations, but they are never systematized and are without a coherent theme. Disorganized schizophrenia manifests with a poor premorbid personality structure, shows an early and sudden onset of the illness, and produces a chronic course without significant remission.

Catatonic schizophrenia was named for the unusual motoric disturbances seen in this group of patients. Their severe psychomotor disturbances range from negativism, mutism, and rigidity, to a dangerously excitable and agitated state. Movements and mannerisms become stereotyped, and the patient may experience periods of extreme stupor in which a state of waxy flexibility is observed. Some catatonic patients may rapidly alternate between extremes of stupor and excitement, posing an unpredictable threat to themselves or others. As these abnormal motor states can last for extended periods of time, the catatonic individual may become malnourished, exhausted, or develop an extremely high temperature. While catatonic schizophrenia was common many years ago, it is now rare.

Undifferentiated schizophrenia is diagnosed if all DSM-IV-TR criterion A symptoms are present but the clinical picture does not fit any of the three subtypes already described.

The **residual schizophrenia** subtype is used to classify those individuals with a history of at least one schizophrenic episode and some residual signs of the disorder, but no active psychotic symptoms. Examples of 'residual signs' of the disorder may include features resembling negative symptoms, such as emotional blunting and social withdrawal, or positive symptoms, including illogical thoughts, eccentric behaviour, and a loosening of associations. If delusions and hallucinations are present, they are relatively mild and have little affect associated with them.

The schizophrenia spectrum

Schizophrenia is a baffling disorder with a bewildering array of symptoms. The disorder's **heterogeneity**, or lack of uniformity from one individual to the next, allows schizophrenia to avoid simple explanation, and the similarity of schizophrenia to the psychoses elicited by a variety of medical conditions and drugs of abuse further hinders our efforts to understand this illness. In the 1960s, Seymour Kety was one of the first to propose that schizophrenia, as it was strictly defined, represented one condition along a spectrum of mental disorders with varying degrees of severity. By viewing schizophrenia not as an all-or-nothing trait but as a highly graded one, Kety provided a framework in which the vulnerability to schizophrenia-like symptoms could vary over a wide range of values, from the totally unaffected individual to the severely impaired individual with various schizophrenia subtypes. The spectrum concept illustrates, at the level of clinical presentation, the causal theories of the disorder that also emerged during this time. In a model first proposed by Irving Gottesman and James Shields—the **multifactorial polygenic (MFP) model**—some degree of unobservable vulnerability to schizophrenia is supposed to be present in all individuals. In this model, the degree of vulnerability is determined by the small, additive effects of a number of genetic and environmental risk factors. If the number of factors possessed by any given individual is beyond some threshold level, then that person will develop schizophrenia; if the threshold level is not reached, full schizophrenia is avoided but some schizophrenia-like symptoms may be evident in milder form. If no genetic or environmental risk factors are present, the individual shows no signs of any abnormalities along the schizophrenia spectrum.

The MFP model has received substantial support in the research literature, and is consistent with observations of higher risk for psychiatric disorders among the relatives of individuals with schizophrenia. Specifically, the relatives of individuals with schizophrenia also have a higher prevalence of schizophrenia-like psychoses, including schizoaffective disorder, schizophreniform disorder, and other psychotic disorders, as well as several personality disorders whose clinical presentations are similar to—but less severe than—schizophrenia, such as schizotypal personality disorder, paranoid personality disorder, and schizoid personality disorder.

Two lines of evidence have been used to define schizophrenia spectrum disorders. The first is that a disorder should show some clinical similarity to schizophrenia. For example, the suspiciousness of a person with paranoid personality disorder is not delusional, but is similar to a paranoid delusion. The second criterion for inclusion in the schizophrenia spectrum is that a disorder should be more common in families having a member with schizophrenia than in other families. The idea here is that the family member with schizophrenia has a 'full dose' of schizophrenia genes and environmental risk factors, but the member with a spectrum disorder only has a 'mild dose'.

Schizoaffective disorder

According to DSM-IV-TR's diagnostic standards, schizoaffective disorder has many symptoms in common with schizophrenia, along with symptoms of unusually high or low mood. In fact, the diagnostic criteria for schizoaffective disorder specify that criterion A of schizophrenia must be satisfied and that delusions or hallucinations must be present. Thus, schizoaffective disorder shares more in common with schizophrenia clinically than any other disorder. Of the two subtypes of schizoaffective disorder, the depressive type is thought to lie nearer the schizophrenia spectrum, while the bipolar type is thought to have causes that are closer to that of bipolar disorder; however, there is evidence that both subtypes are on a disease continuum that includes schizophrenia, suggesting that the traditional boundary between schizophrenia and mood disorders may be somewhat artificial and unjustified.

Dozens of family-based genetic studies (including twin and adoption studies) have found a higher-than-average rate of schizoaffective disorder among the biological (but not adoptive) relatives of individuals with schizophrenia, which underscores the importance of a genetic relationship between schizophrenia and schizoaffective disorder. The rate of schizoaffective disorder among family members of people with schizophrenia may be as high as 9%, which is well above the rates of schizoaffective disorder in the general population (less than 1%).

Psychotic disorder, not otherwise specified

In practise, it is not uncommon to come across patients who are psychotic but do not meet the criteria for schizophrenia or the other differential diagnostic categories mentioned above. Many of these individuals will be diagnosed as having psychotic disorder, not otherwise specified (**NOS**), which is a residual category reserved for such patients. Examples of psychosis NOS are transient psychotic episodes associated with the menstrual cycle, persistent auditory hallucinations as the only disturbance, some 'postpartum psychoses,' and psychoses with confusing or unusual clinical features. Some patients with psychotic disorder, NOS will eventually be diagnosed with schizophrenia as their disorder evolves.

Schizophreniform disorder

Individuals who meet criteria A, D, and E for schizophrenia but have only exhibited symptoms for 1–6 months may receive a diagnosis of schizophreniform disorder. Because individuals with schizophreniform disorder meet several diagnostic criteria for schizophrenia, the differential diagnosis of these two related disorders is impractical. Instead, many cases of schizophreniform disorder are coded as 'provisional,' meaning that the individual has had symptoms for only 1–6 months but may continue to exhibit symptoms that may eventually qualify the patient for a different diagnosis, such as schizophrenia.

Schizotypal personality disorder

Of several personality disorders that have clinical features in common with schizophrenia, schizotypal personality disorder is the most similar in terms of the number of shared criteria and the degree of impairment. This is due in part to the fact that the diagnosis of schizotypal personality disorder is based upon the presence of both social and cognitive deficits, which are also central to the diagnosis of schizophrenia itself. In fact, the features of schizotypal personality disorder reflect those of schizophrenia, but with less severity. For example, the ideas of reference, odd beliefs, magical thinking, unusual perceptual experiences, and suspiciousness that characterize schizotypal personality disorder are milder forms of the delusions and hallucinations of paranoid schizophrenia, while the odd thinking, speech, and behaviour of this personality disorder resemble the analogous—but more severe—features of disorganized schizophrenia. Furthermore, the appearance of affective disturbance, the lack of close friends, and the excessive social anxiety commonly seen in schizotypal personality disorder are easily recognizable as diluted forms of the essential social dysfunction of schizophrenia.

Paranoid personality disorder

Patients with paranoid personality disorder have a pervasive distrust and suspiciousness of others, where malevolent motives are ascribed to others without sufficient basis. Although paranoid personality disorder as a whole shares only this single group of symptoms with schizophrenia, these features are central to the diagnosis of paranoid-type schizophrenia; thus, the inclusion of paranoid personality disorder into the group of schizophrenia spectrum disorders seems warranted.

Schizoid personality disorder

In the same vein, there also appears to be good reason to include schizoid personality disorder in the group of schizophrenia spectrum disorders. The principal clinical feature of schizoid personality disorder is a consistent pattern of social dysfunction ranging from aversion of social relationships to restricted affective expression in interpersonal settings, symptoms that are similar to (but less severe than) the social dysfunction that is a fundamental feature of schizophrenia.

Non-psychotic schizophrenia spectrum conditions have also been studied in this manner to determine their familial clustering with schizophrenia. Several studies have shown that some relatives of individuals with schizophrenia have maladaptive personality traits, such as impaired interpersonal relationships, social anxiety, and constricted emotional responses. Less frequently, mild forms of thought disorder, suspiciousness, magical thinking, illusions, and perceptual aberrations have been observed. This composite set of personality characteristics points to elevated rates of schizotypal, schizoid, and/or paranoid personality disorders among the relatives of patients with schizophrenia.

Among these disorders, schizotypal personality disorder shows the strongest familial link with schizophrenia, with rates of the personality disorder 1.5–5 times higher among the relatives of patients with schizophrenia than in the relatives of controls or in the general population. Furthermore, adoption studies show that schizotypal personality disorder has not only a familial relationship with schizophrenia but also a truly genetic link.

Investigations of paranoid and schizoid personality disorders have not provided a similar level of evidence for a familial association with schizophrenia. In fact, more than one study has found no increase in the rate of paranoid personality disorder among the first-degree relatives of individuals with schizophrenia when compared to the rates observed in the family members of control subjects. Schizoid personality disorder has been found to have a slightly stronger relationship with schizophrenia, but the evidence for familial aggregation with schizophrenia is still weak overall. Based on the superficial similarities of these two personality disorders to schizophrenia, it is indeed surprising that neither disorder shows a stronger genetic etiologic relationship to schizophrenia.

It is interesting to note that the evidence for inclusion in the schizophrenia spectrum is strongest for those disorders that share the most clinical features with schizophrenia (e.g., schizoaffective disorder and schizotypal personality disorder); however, at such an early stage in this field of study, the observed relationship may be no more than an artefact of the much greater level of research attention that has been devoted to the analysis of these two disorders relative to schizoid and paranoid personality disorders, or due to the relatively low prevalence of the latter two conditions. As paranoid and schizoid personality disorders are more extensively examined for familial links with schizophrenia, and as more subjects with these conditions become available for study, these conditions may be found to cluster at a higher, lower, or comparable frequency than schizoaffective disorder and schizotypal personality disorder in families that are affected by schizophrenia.

Differential diagnosis of other psychotic disorders

Psychotic disorder due to a general medical condition

A diagnosis of schizophrenia should only be arrived at after careful exclusion of any non-psychiatric medical conditions that can be detected through clinical examination, collection of medical history, or laboratory findings. Schizophrenia-like psychosis is more common in individuals who experience a closed head injury, for example, and the trauma need not be suffered by any particular brain region; rather, a brain injury of any type may precipitate such symptoms. Other medical conditions, such as temporal lobe epilepsy, can produce symptoms, such as frank psychosis, that very closely resemble those of schizophrenia.

Substance-induced psychotic disorder

As in the general population, drug abuse has become increasingly common among psychiatric patients over the last four decades. Because so many licit and illicit substances evoke behaviours that are similar to symptoms of schizophrenia, especially psychosis, the differential diagnosis of substance abuse and schizophrenia based solely on clinical presentation is exceedingly difficult. Although the differences between substance-induced psychoses and the psychosis of schizophrenia are subtle, progress has been made in establishing criteria that may distinguish between the two. For example, amphetamine psychosis can be differentiated from paranoid schizophrenia by both the prominence of visual hallucinations and the relative absence of thought disorder in the former. Compared with schizophrenia, amphetamine psychosis is also more likely to manifest distortion of body image. Other reports, however, suggest that the most common features of amphetamine psychosis are indistinguishable from schizophrenia, so this continues to be an area of active research and debate.

The psychosis produced by the use of lysergic acid (LSD), like that seen with amphetamine, can be differentiated from the psychotic features of schizophrenia based on the increased prevalence of visual hallucinations, and can also be distinguished based on the presence of mystical preoccupation and subtle gaps in logic. LSD-induced and schizophrenic psychoses can further be discriminated by more conceptual disorganization and excitement, along with less motor retardation and blunt affect, in the drug-induced state. However, just as some have found amphetamine-induced and schizophrenic psychoses to be indistinguishable, some researchers have challenged the generality of any distinctions between LSD-induced psychosis and that of schizophrenia. Attempts have also been made to distinguish between the psychotic symptoms of schizophrenia and the effects of the dissociative compound phencyclidine (PCP), again with mixed results.

A comprehensive review of the available literature suggests that typical substance-induced psychoses are not identical to typical examples of schizophrenia, but that individual features of the two are remarkably similar. Thus, despite the best efforts of many researchers, it is quite clear that reliance on symptoms alone is not adequate for differentiating drug-induced conditions that resemble schizophrenia from the disorder itself. When drug histories are unreliable, or when multiple drugs have been abused, the dissection of clinical features will be even less useful in deriving an accurate diagnosis. Furthermore, if the duration of the drug-induced psychotic episode exceeds the duration of drug action, the discriminating power of the criteria outlined above will be quite low. However, if the patient's prior history is relatively normal and the duration of psychosis does not exceed the duration of drug action, then it is reasonable to assume the psychosis is substance-induced. We have found that psychotic drug abusers having psychotic symptoms that exceed the duration of drug action but persisting less than 6 months have better pre-psychosis personalities, shorter hospitalization, less need for pharmacotherapy, better discharge dispositions, and lower familial risks for psychiatric disorders than do psychotic drug abusers whose psychoses exceed 6 months in duration. Thus, it appears that the effective differential diagnosis of schizophrenia and substance-induced psychoses requires adequate observations of the course of the disorder.

Delusional disorder

Although delusional (paranoid) disorder is a rare condition, it is easily confused with paranoid schizophrenia and so must be carefully differentiated from this schizophrenia subtype. Delusional disorder comprises a group of syndromes in which the delusion is the critical shared element; however, individuals with this disorder do not meet criterion A for schizophrenia. Generally, the affected individual's delusions are well systematized and logically developed. Prior to the DSM-IV, delusional disorder was called paranoid disorder, but this transition represents the evolution of the diagnostic category to include delusions in which persecution or jealousy is not the main focus. In the differential diagnosis of delusional disorder and paranoid schizophrenia, it is critical to establish the presence or absence of hallucinations. Hallucinations may be a feature of paranoid schizophrenia but are not associated with delusional disorder. Delusional disorder can be further differentiated from paranoid schizophrenia based on the absence of positive symptoms in the former, with the exception of the delusion. In further contrast with paranoid schizophrenia, the delusions experienced by the delusional-disordered patient are typically somewhat plausible and not bizarre.

Brief psychotic disorder

The diagnosis of brief psychotic disorder is appropriate for patients exhibiting classic symptoms of schizophrenia that persist for only a restricted period of time. To qualify for this diagnosis, symptoms such as disorganized speech, disordered behaviour, delusions, or hallucinations may only be present for a period of time between 1 day and 1 month in duration. Brief psychotic disorder is usually precipitated by a profoundly stressful event, in response to which the patient becomes overwhelmed with emotional turmoil or confusion. Although the symptoms of this disorder persist for only a limited amount of time, this condition can be severely debilitating, and can place the patient at increased risk for harm due to the cognitive impairment, delusional thought structure, and faulty judgement imposed by the disorder. In some cases of brief psychotic disorder, the existence of a personality disorder similar to the schizophrenic prodrome may suggest schizophrenia. Careful examination of the personality structure and observation of the clinical course will clarify this distinction.

Shared psychotic disorder

If a patient presents with a delusion similar in content to one that has been previously established in another individual, a diagnosis of shared psychotic disorder may be issued. In many cases of shared psychotic disorder, the two patients are related to one another and, in their relationship, the first one to become psychotic is often the dominant member of the dyad. Shared psychoses usually occur between two individuals, which is why this disorder is also known as *folie à deux*, but they may also occur among members of a large group.

Mood disorders

Differentiating between schizophrenia and major mood disorders with psychotic features can be difficult. Hallucinations and delusions are experienced by many manic and depressed patients, and these features can resemble those of schizophrenia. The two disorders are differentiated in the DSM-IV-TR based on the duration of the manic or depressive episode. Thus, if the affective state is not short in duration relative to the length of time that schizophrenia criterion A symptoms are present during both the active and residual phases of the illness, a mood disorder is indicated. Of course, determining the relative duration that a set of symptoms has been present in the course of an illness can be difficult.

To assist the differential diagnosis of schizophrenia and mood disorders beyond the criteria laid out above, the clinician can examine the content of the patient's hallucinations and/or delusions. If these psychotic features conform to the patient's affective state, a mood disorder is suspected. For example, manic patients often have grandiose delusions, and depressed patients often have delusions of sin or guilt. The content of auditory hallucinations may also conform to affective states, and if undertones of elation or despair are detected, these can also assist in this differential diagnosis. If the affective tone of hallucinations and delusions are ambiguous or uninformative, and if the patient cannot be clearly diagnosed with either schizophrenia or a mood disorder based on other criteria, a diagnosis of schizoaffective disorder is appropriate.

The most efficient way to minimize the improper classification of other disorders as schizophrenia is to collect all the available data on each patient and to recognize that no clinical feature is entirely characteristic of the disorder.

If, based on a thorough clinical interview, the diagnosis of a psychotic patient remains unclear, it is sometimes useful to collect information about psychiatric illness in biological relatives. Although family psychiatric history is not considered a diagnostic criterion in DSM-IV-TR, family, twin, and adoption studies suggest that a psychotic individual with relatives affected by schizophrenia is more likely to have schizophrenia, whereas one with manic or depressed relatives is likely to have a mood disorder.

Upcoming changes in the diagnosis of schizophrenia and schizophrenia spectrum disorders

A major revision of the DSM is underway, and will culminate in the next edition, DSM-V, in approximately May 2013. The purpose of this revision is to update the manual based on our evolving understanding of schizophrenia and other disorders, but also to bring the DSM criteria more in line with the other major diagnostic and classification system used by much of the world, the World Health Organization's ICD system, which is presently in its tenth edition. The proposed changes to DSM-IV-TR criteria are substantial, including the proposed abolition of all five schizophrenia subtypes (catatonic, disorganized, paranoid, residual, and undifferentiated). The rationale for the proposed removal of subtypes from DSM-V is multifaceted, including the fact that the subtype designations are not routinely used in clinical practise and, more importantly, that these (nor any currently advocated subtyping schemes for schizophrenia) are more heuristic than valid. Until valid subtypes are derived by further scientific research, the committee establishing DSM-V diagnoses and criteria is favouring exclusion of all schizophrenia subtypes. In reality, however, some subtypes of the disorder (such as paranoid schizophrenia) seem to have face validity and may persist in the common and clinical vernacular for some time.

Beyond this proposed change, the diagnostic criteria for schizophrenia itself are not slated to undergo major revision in DSM-V. In fact, diagnostic criteria B–F will likely be unchanged from DSM-IV-TR, with only minor clarifications imparted to criterion A. The minor changes in criterion A are as follows: 1) disorganized behaviour is removed from the grouping of grossly disorganized and catatonic behaviour, as catatonic behaviour is a motor sign whereas disorganization constitutes its own psychopathological domain; 2) negative symptoms have been clarified with regard to 'restricted' affect rather than 'flat' affect; also, avolition/asociality and restricted affect are now described as distinguishable dimensions of negative symptoms; 3) the requirement of only one characteristic symptom in the presence of a bizarre delusion or hallucination has been eliminated; and 4) at least one of the characteristic symptoms (delusions, hallucinations, or disorganized speech) must be present.

The diagnoses of several schizophrenia spectrum disorders will also change in DSM-V. For example, the symptoms in category A of schizophreniform disorder will change equivalently to the change proposed in category A of schizophrenia itself. Changes are also planned to clarify the language regarding a diagnosis of schizoaffective disorder, requiring clinicians to develop more clarity and certainty in the patient expressing both psychotic and mood disturbances of sufficient severity to warrant the diagnosis. These changes are intended to make the diagnosis of schizoaffective disorder more reliable, and may also lead to a lower rate of diagnosis of this already rare disorder.

Another interesting change that may come about in DSM-V is the proposed use of dimensional assessments in diagnosing. As we have described above, the wide range of deficits seen in individuals with schizophrenia can vary along an axis of severity. The new version of DSM proposes that the severity of these deficits should be ancillary information to accompany the diagnostic judgement of a disorder. The domains proposed for inclusion are: hallucinations, delusions, disorganization, abnormal psychomotor behaviour, restricted emotional expression, avolition, impaired cognition, depression, and mania. Each category of severity would be assessed on a four-point scale with reference to the last month.

A watershed event for the field would be the inclusion of a psychosis-risk diagnosis in the new version of DSM-V, which is presently being considered. This diagnosis would be given in situations where an individual exhibits all of the following: 1) delusions, hallucinations, or disorganized speech in attenuated form with intact reality testing, but of sufficient severity and/or frequency that it is not discounted or ignored; 2) symptoms must be present in the past month and occur at an average frequency of at least once per week in the past month; 3) symptoms must have begun in or significantly worsened in the past year; 4) symptoms are sufficiently distressing and disabling to the patient and/or parent/guardian to lead them to seek help; 5) symptoms are not better explained by any DSM-V diagnosis, including substance-related disorder; and 6) clinical criteria for any DSM-V psychotic disorder have never been met. This designation could have important individual and public health benefits, because the identification of the at-risk or prodromal state as a real clinical entity might allow treatment to commence sooner, leading to a better prognosis.

5

How common is schizophrenia?

➡ Key points

♦ International studies show that, with a few exceptions, the prevalence of schizophrenia is similar around the world—between 0.5 and 0.8%.

♦ In reporting the distribution of schizophrenia, the term 'incidence rate' is used when estimating the number of new cases in a year. 'Prevalence rate' is used when both old and new cases are looked at together over a short period of time.

♦ When looking at the 'lifetime risk' associated with schizophrenia, persons older than 39 have largely passed the risk period, those younger than 20 have largely not yet entered the risk period, and those between 20 and 39 fall within the greatest risk period. Depending on the diagnostic criteria used, lifetime risk ranges from 0.3% to 3.7%. It is generally considered to be approximately 1%, meaning that 1 in 100 people will develop schizophrenia in their lifetime.

The prevalence of schizophrenia (i.e., the number of affected individuals in the population) has been estimated at least 42 times in 19 different countries (Table 5.1). The prevalence estimates obtained from these studies are remarkably consistent, despite the cultural heterogeneity of the samples and the methodological diversity of the studies. These results clearly indicate that schizophrenia is not specific to one type of culture, and that the disorder does not discriminate between East and West or between developed and less-developed countries. The lowest estimate of schizophrenia's prevalence was

Table 5.1 Prevalence of schizophrenia

Study	Location	Prevalence per 1000
Brugger (1931)	Germany	2.4
Brugger (1933)	Germany	2.2
Klemperer (1933)	Germany	10.0
Strömgren (1935)	Denmark	3.3
Lemkao (1936)	USA	2.9
Roth and Luton (1938)	USA	1.7
Brugger (1938)	Germany	2.3
Lin (1946–1948)	China	2.1
Mayer-Gross (1948)	Scotland	4.2
Bremer (1951)	Norway	4.4
Böök (1953)	Sweden	9.5
Larson (1954)	Sweden	4.6
National Survey (1954)	Japan	2.3
Essen-Möller (1956)	Sweden	6.7
Yoo (1961)	Korea	3.8
Juel-Nielsen (1962)	Denmark	1.5
Ivanys (1963)	Czechoslovakia	1.7
Krasik (1965)	USSR	3.1
Hagnell (1966)	Sweden	4.5
Wing (1967)	England	4.4
	Scotland	2.5
	USA	7.0
Lin (1969)	Taiwan	1.4
Jayasundera (1969)	Ceylon	3.2
Kato (1969)	Japan	2.3
Dube (1970)	India	3.7
Roy (1970)	Canada	
	Indians	5.7
	Non-Indians	1.6
Crocetti (1971)	Yugoslavia	
	Rijeka	7.3
	Zagreb	4.2
Kulcar (1971)	Yugoslavia	
	Lubin	7.4
	Sinj-Trogir	2.9
Bash (1972)	Iran	2.1

(Continued)

Table 5.1 Prevalence of schizophrenia (*Continued*)

Study	Location	Prevalence per 1000
Zharikov (1972)	USSR	5.1
Babigian (1975)	USA	4.7
Temkov (1975)	Bulgaria	2.8
Rotstein (1977)	USSR	3.8
Nielsen (1977)	Denmark	2.7
Ouspenskaya (1978)	USSR	5.3
Böök (1978)	Sweden	17.0
Lehtinen (1978)	Finland	15.0
Wijesinghe (1978)	Ceylon	5.6
Weissman (1980)	New Haven	4.0
Hafner (1980)	Germany	1.2
Walsh (1980)	Ireland	8.3
Rin (1982)	Taiwan	0.9
Sikanartey (1984)	Ghana	0.6
Meyers (1984)	USA	
	New Haven	11.0
	Baltimore	10.0
	St Louis	6.0
Von Korff (1985)	Baltimore	6.0
Hwu (1989)	Taiwan	2.4
Astrup (1989)	Norway	7.3
Hwu (1989)	Taiwan	2.4
Bøjholm (1989)	Denmark	3.3
Lee (1990)	Korea	3.1
Stefánsson (1991)	Iceland	3.0
Youssef (1991)	Ireland	3.3
Chen (1993)	China	1.3
de Salvia (1993)	Italy	1.4
Kendler (1994)	Ireland	5.3
Jeffreys (1997)	UK	5.1
Myles-Worsley (1999)	Palau	19.9
Waldo (1999)	Micronesia	6.8
Kebede (1999)	Ethiopia	7.1
Nimgaonkar (2000)	Canada	1.2
Jablensky (2000)	Australia	4.5

0.6 cases per 1000 people sampled in Ghana, and the highest prevalence was measured in Sweden, where 17.0 cases per 1000 were measured in one sample. The unusually high prevalence of 17.0 per 1000 reported in this Swedish sample by Böök *et al.* (1978) may be caused by special environmental factors. The population studied was a north Swedish isolate separated from the rest of the country and located in an austere environment. It has been suggested that such environments may be more conducive to the withdrawn, isolated lifestyle preferred by many individuals with schizophrenia.

When considered as a whole, the studies listed in Table 5.1 indicate that 0.5% of the population suffers from a schizophrenic disorder at any given point in time. However, the prevalence estimates presented in Table 5.1 may actually underestimate the lifetime risk for schizophrenia, since recovered cases are counted as unaffected and no correction is made for the variable age of onset of the disorder. As seen in Table 5.2, the lifetime risk for schizophrenia has been estimated at between 0.3% and 2.7%, with a mean of approximately 1.0%. Thus, one of every 100 individuals can be expected to develop schizophrenia at some point in their life, according to the best available estimate of the population prevalence.

It is also very useful to know the incidence of schizophrenia, which is the number of new cases of the disorder that emerge over a period of time. Estimates of schizophrenia incidence in nine different countries vary from a low of 0.10 per 1000 to a high of 0.69 per 1000, with an average of 0.35 new cases of schizophrenia per 1000 individuals in a given population (Table 5.3). Based on such incidence estimates, it has been noted that lifetime prevalence figures are lower than expected, especially since the illness is usually chronic, but this can be reconciled based on the two-fold increase in early death among people with schizophrenia relative to the general population.

The figures for lifetime risk estimated by the above method should be used with caution. Since the death rate for people with schizophrenia is higher than that for the general population, the figure may be an underestimate: deceased people with schizophrenia cannot be counted. In addition to the higher death rate, those people with schizophrenia who have recovered or who are in remission cannot be detected. The lifetime risk rates for schizophrenia are more variable across studies than are the prevalence or incidence rates. This is probably due to methodological differences in how the rates are computed. The difference in the magnitudes of the prevalence, incidence, and lifetime risk rates underscores the importance of using these terms correctly. As our discussion clearly indicates, the risk for developing schizophrenia over one's lifetime is much higher then either the incidence or prevalence of the disease.

Table 5.2 Lifetime prevalence of schizophrenia

Study	Country	Lifetime prevalence per 1000
Hagnell (1966)	Sweden	14.0
Brugger (1931)	Germany	3.8
Brugger (1933)	Germany	4.1
Klemperer (1933)	Germany	14.0
Brugger (1938)	Germany	3.6
Strömgren (1938)	Denmark	5.8
Ødegard (1946)	Norway	18.7
Fremming (1947)	Denmark	9.0
Böök (1953)	Sweden	26.6
Sjögren (1954)	Sweden	16.0
Helgason (1964)	Iceland	8.0
Helgason (1977)	Iceland	4.9
Böök (1978)	Sweden	24.8
Robins (1984)	USA	19.0
	New Haven	19.0
	Baltimore	16.0
	St Louis	10.0
Widerlov (1989)	Denmark	37.0
Hwu (1989)	Taiwan	2.6
Lehtinen (1990)	Finland	13.0
Youssef (1991)	Ireland	6.4
Bijl (1998)	The Netherlands	4.0
Thavichachart (2001)	Thailand	13.0

As of 2004, according to the World Health Organization (WHO), an estimated 26.3 million people worldwide were affected with schizophrenia. While not a leading cause of death, schizophrenia ranked 14th among conditions responsible for moderate to severe disability, with 16.7 million people at this level of disability globally. The majority of these (65%) were under the age of 60. Not surprisingly, countries defined by WHO to be low- or middle-income (i.e., having a gross national income per capita < $10,066) had a disproportionate share (84%) of this group.

Table 5.3 Incidence of schizophrenia

Study	Country	Annual number of new cases per 1000
Ødegaard (1946)	Norway	0.24
Hollingshead (1958)	USA	0.30
Norris (1959)	UK	0.17
Jaco (1960)	USA	0.35
Dunham (1965)	USA	0.52
Warthen (1967)	USA	0.70
Adelstein (1968)	UK	0.26–0.35
Walsh (1969)	Ireland	0.46–0.57
Hafner (1970)	Germany	0.54
Lieberman (1974)	USSR	0.19–0.20
Hailey (1974)	UK	0.10–0.14
Babigian (1975)	USA	0.69
Nielsen (1976)	Denmark	0.20
Helgason (1977)	Iceland	0.27
Krupinski (1983)	Australia	0.18
Folnegovic (1990)	Croatia	0.22
Youssef (1991)	Ireland	0.16
Jablensky (1992)	Colombia	0.09
Folnegovic (1990)	Croatia	0.22
Jablensky (1992)	USA	0.12
Jablensky (1992)	USA	0.13
Jablensky (1992)	UK	0.19
Jablensky (1992)	Russia	0.15
Jablensky (1992)	Nigeria	0.11
Jablensky (1992)	Japan	0.16
Jablensky (1992)	Ireland	0.16
Jablensky (1992)	India	0.25
Jablensky (1992)	Denmark	0.13
Jablensky (1992)	Czech Republic	0.08
Nicole (1992)	Canada	0.20
McNaught (1997)	UK	0.21
Preti (2000)	Italy	0.88
Rajkumar (1993)	India	0.41
Mahy (1999)	Barbados	0.32
Hickling (1991)	Jamaica	0.24
Svedberg (2001)	Sweden	0.17
Hanoeman (2002)	Surinam	0.16

To provide a sense of the burden of this disease, the WHO has calculated a measure, called the disability-adjusted life year (DALY), which 'can be thought of as one lost year of "healthy" life' due to death or disability. Using this metric, the low- and middle-income countries are seen to be carrying an even greater burden for this disease, accounting for 91% of the years of healthy life lost to schizophrenia.

6

Is schizophrenia inherited?

➔ Key points

♦ Family studies show that schizophrenia runs in families. The lifetime risk for the siblings and children of schizophrenic patients is anywhere between 4 and 14%, averaging ten times higher than that of the general population.

♦ Identical twins come from the same fertilized egg, whereas fraternal twins come from different fertilized eggs but share the same perinatal uterine environment. Thus, identical twins are 100% similar genetically, whereas fraternal twins are 50% similar. If one twin has schizophrenia, the probability of the other twin also having schizophrenia is 53% for identical twins and 15% for fraternal twins. This shows that schizophrenia is not strictly a genetic disease, but has a strong genetic component.

♦ Adoption studies show that schizophrenia is transmitted to the biological relatives of patients, not the adoptive relatives. This suggests that familial transmission is due to genes, not learning or bad parenting.

♦ Some genes for schizophrenia have been discovered, but most of the genes that cause the disorder are unknown.

We have known for some time, from family studies done in Europe in the first half of the twentieth century, that schizophrenia runs in families. These studies found the risks for the parents, brothers, and sisters of schizophrenic patients to be between 4 and 14%—on average about 10 times as high as that for the general population. For children of schizophrenic patients, the risk was 12.3%, nearly 15 times the general population risk. When both parents had schizophrenia, the risk increased to about 40%. The risk to uncles and aunts, nephews and nieces, grandchildren, and half-brothers or -sisters was roughly three times the general population risk. This was considerably lower than the risk to the relatives in the immediate family circle. On the whole, these pioneering studies demonstrated that the closer the blood relationship of a person to an individual with schizophrenia, the higher the risk of schizophrenia.

Contemporary studies using more rigorous research methods and narrower, criterion-based definitions of schizophrenia also found schizophrenia to run in families. However, they report risk figures that are somewhat lower than those found in earlier studies. For example, in a large family study from Iowa, Tsuang and colleagues reported the risk of schizophrenia to brothers and sisters of individuals with schizophrenia to be approximately 3%. Although smaller than the early European studies, it was five times greater than the risk to relatives of persons without schizophrenia. Other contemporary studies also reported risk estimates approximately one-third of those obtained by the earlier European studies. Diagnostic practises appear to play a strong role in these different risk estimates. The early European studies tended to use a fairly broad definition of the illness whereas the contemporary studies used a stringent criterion-based diagnosis developed for research purposes. Indeed, contemporary researchers have noted that their family risk figures for schizophrenia are similar to the figures obtained by the earlier European studies when atypical cases are included in the definition of schizophrenia.

Although these family patterns suggest an hereditary basis for schizophrenia, they could also be explained on the basis of shared environment. Thus, some traits that run in families, like eye colour, are determined by genes, but others, such as one's spoken language, are learned and not due to genes. In order to disentangle heredity and environment, information from other sources is needed. The results from twin and adoption studies are used for this purpose.

Twin studies

There are two types of twins: monozygotic (or identical) and dizygotic (or fraternal). Identical twins come from one fertilized egg and therefore they have identical sets of genes. Fraternal twins come from two different fertilized eggs and therefore share only half their genes on average; they resemble ordinary brothers and sisters except that they shared the same uterine environment before birth. Within a twin-pair, if both twins have schizophrenia, they are said to be concordant for schizophrenia; if one has schizophrenia and the other is not schizophrenic, they are called discordant.

If schizophrenia were due entirely to genetic factors, the concordance rates for identical twins and fraternal twin pairs would be 100% and 50%, respectively. In the absence of complete genetic determination, evidence for a strong genetic component in schizophrenia would be given by a significantly higher concordance rate for schizophrenia in identical twin pairs than fraternal twin pairs. On the other hand, if schizophrenia were entirely due to environmental factors, there would be no difference between the concordance rates of identical and fraternal twin pairs, since both types of twin pairs have a common environment.

By pooling the results of twin studies from different parts of the world, concordance rates of about 53% for identical twin pairs and 15% for fraternal twin pairs have been found. This can be taken as evidence of the presence of an hereditary component in schizophrenia. The fact that the concordance rate for identical twin pairs is not 100% indicates that factors other than heredity are involved.

Twin studies of schizophrenia have been criticized on the grounds that being raised as a twin may confuse self-identity, particularly in identical twin pairs where one twin can easily be taken for the other. However, if confusion of self-identity leads to higher concordance of the rate of schizophrenia in identical twins, one would expect to find a higher risk of schizophrenia in identical twins than in the general population, but this is not the case.

Another explanation for the higher concordance in identical than fraternal twin pairs is that the former are exposed to more similar predisposing environmental factors than the latter. This hypothesis can be tested by looking at twin partners separated at birth and raised in different environments. A high concordance rate for identical twin pairs reared apart would refute the theory that sharing the same predisposing environment leads to the higher concordance rate in identical twin pairs. Greater than half of such identical twin pairs have been reported to be concordant for schizophrenia.

In spite of the methodological problems involved in twin studies, on the whole they provide evidence for the presence of a strong hereditary component in schizophrenia.

Adoption studies

More evidence for the role of hereditary factors in schizophrenia comes from adoption studies. In the 1960s, pioneering adoption studies were carried out in the USA and Denmark. In the USA, Dr Leonard Heston examined 47 children in Oregon who had been separated from their biological schizophrenic mothers within 3 days of birth. These children were raised by adoptive parents with whom they had no biological relationship. He also examined a control group of 50 persons who had been separated from their non-schizophrenic mothers.

The idea behind the study was to see if children born to schizophrenic mothers would have a higher probability of developing schizophrenia than children born to non-schizophrenic mothers, when no member of either group had been exposed to his or her mother or to any other biological relative. If genes cause schizophrenia then the biological children of schizophrenic mothers should have a higher risk for schizophrenia regardless of who raised them as children. In contrast, if the parenting relationship causes schizophrenia, then separating children from a schizophrenic parent should prevent them from developing schizophrenia. Dr Heston's results were clear: five children of schizophrenic mothers became schizophrenic, but none of the children of non-schizophrenic mothers became schizophrenic. This provided convincing evidence for the hereditary basis of schizophrenia.

In Denmark, where excellent national and medical databases are available, Dr Seymour Kety and colleagues from the US National Institute of Mental Health along with Dr Fini Schulsinger from Denmark carried out adoption studies of schizophrenia. In the Greater Copenhagen area a total of 5500 children were separated from their biological families by adoption between 1923 and 1947. Of these children, 33 who later developed schizophrenia were studied along with 33 non-schizophrenic adoptees. The investigators examined the biological relatives of these schizophrenic and non-schizophrenic adoptees. To eliminate any possible bias in making the diagnosis, all relatives studied were examined by investigators who did not know if they came from a schizophrenic or non-schizophrenic adoptee.

Drs Kety and Schulsinger diagnosed 21% of the biological relatives of schizophrenic patients with schizophrenia or a related disorder, compared with 11% of the biological relatives of non-schizophrenics. They found no differences in rates of schizophrenia between the adoptive relatives of the schizophrenic and non-schizophrenic adoptees. The findings provided additional, strong evidence for the genetic basis of schizophrenia.

One component of the Danish study was similar to Dr Heston's American study. Children born to schizophrenic families but raised by non-schizophrenic families were compared with children born to, and raised by, non-schizophrenic parents. Consistent with the genetic theory of the disorder, schizophrenia and related disorders were found in 32% of the former group but only in 18% of the latter group.

The adoption studies discussed up till now clearly show that schizophrenic parents transmit the liability towards schizophrenia to their children even when these children are reared by non-schizophrenic parents. This directly shows that biological relationships predict the risk for schizophrenia and indirectly suggests that parenting does not cause schizophrenia. Fortunately, the

Danish samples provided a direct test of whether being raised by a schizophrenic parent could cause schizophrenia.

This direct test was possible because the Danish sample included some persons who had been born of non-schizophrenic parents but raised by a schizophrenic parent. If being reared by a schizophrenic parent caused schizophrenia, then these persons should be likely to suffer from schizophrenia. This was not the case. The investigators concluded that rearing by a schizophrenic parent was not a significant cause of schizophrenia in a child who was not genetically predisposed to the disorder.

Findings from adoption studies thus strengthen the case that genes cause the transmission of schizophrenia in families. However, adoption studies have their limitations. Although the American and Danish investigators tried to disentangle genetic and environmental influences, they did not succeed completely. In a lecture by Dr Kety, it was pointed out that even though an adopted child had been separated from the mother soon after birth, the child had spent 9 months in the mother's uterus and some time with her immediately after the birth. During that time, the mother could have transmitted to the fetus some non-genetic biological or psychosocial factor that might have resulted in the child's schizophrenia many years later.

What factor could cause such delayed effects? One candidate is a slow virus, which could lie dormant for years before being triggered by a combination of biological and psychosocial conditions. If a mother harbored such a virus then she could transmit it to her child while she/he was in her uterus. No such slow virus has been discovered, but the data from family, twin, and adoption studies do not completely exclude the possibility that one might exist.

Fortunately, the Danish researchers could examine whether or not *in utero* influences might have explained the results of their adoption studies. They studied a group of blood relatives who had not been exposed to the same uterine environment. These were half-brothers or -sisters (from the father's side) of children who were given out for adoption and became schizophrenic later. These paternal half-siblings had the same father but different mothers. Dr Kety and colleagues found that 8 of 63 paternal half-siblings of schizophrenic adoptees (12.7%) had schizophrenia on interview compared with only 1 of 64 paternal half-siblings of non-schizophrenic adoptees (1.6%). Because paternal half-siblings have different mothers, these results cannot be explained by *in utero* effects. Indeed, the fact that a higher rate of schizophrenia was found among these half-siblings from the father's side, than in the half-siblings of the controls, gave the most compelling evidence for the hereditary basis of schizophrenia.

The Danish adoption study results were subsequently replicated in another, provincial, Danish sample. Taken together—along with Heston's adoption study and others that subsequently emerged—the Danish work motivated a large scientific effort focused on understanding the mechanism by which the susceptibility towards schizophrenia was genetically transmitted in families.

The mechanism of genetic transmission

Although family, twin, and adoption studies conclusively show that schizophrenia is at least partly caused by genes, it has been surprisingly difficult for researchers to clearly define the mechanism of genetic transmission. Several possibilities exist. At one extreme it may be that a defect in a single gene is the genetic cause of schizophrenia. At the other extreme, each person with schizophrenia may have a 'personal aetiology' that is unique. In between is a scenario where many genes act in combination with one another, and with the environment, to cause the illness.

The transmission of our genes obeys known biological laws and these laws have a clear mathematical description. It is therefore theoretically possible to use the results of family, twin, and adoption studies to determine whether one, several, or very many genes are the cause of schizophrenia. Unfortunately, attempts to fit mathematical genetic models to schizophrenia studies have been contradictory. Some studies support the idea of single-gene transmission, but others find that many genes must exist to explain the pattern of transmission in families.

The frustration felt by scientists unable to describe the mechanism of transmission was initially relieved by rapid developments in the laboratory science of molecular genetics during the 1980s. These developments made it possible for schizophrenia researchers to use a better methodology for finding genes, known as linkage analysis. Although it had been theoretically possible to find genes with linkage analysis for several decades, these new developments made such progress feasible. In fact with the molecular genetic technologies currently available, there is no question that it is possible to find the genes responsible for many disorders. The list of disorders for which there is already an identified genetic source grows every year. This list includes Huntington's disease, Alzheimer's disease, cystic fibrosis, Duchenne's muscular dystrophy, myotonic dystrophy, familial colon cancer, von Recklinhausen neurofibromatosis, and mental retardation due to fragile X syndrome.

Linkage analysis

Linkage analysis is based on biological events that occur when sperm and egg are created. The most important event is the crossing over of chromosomes. Genetic transmission occurs when chromosomes are passed from parents to children. Our chromosomes occur in pairs; one member of the pair comes from our mother and the other from our father. However, these inherited chromosomes are not identical to any of the original chromosomes of our parents. When gametes are formed, the original chromosomes in each parent's pair cross over each other and exchange portions of their genetic material. After multiple crossovers, the resulting two chromosomes each consist of a new combination of genes.

When this process is completed, each sperm and egg contains one chromosome from each of the newly formed pairs. Whether two genes on the same chromosome will remain together or will recombine due to crossing over depends on their distance from one another. Linkage occurs when two genes on the same original chromosome are so close to each other that crossing over rarely or never occurs between them. Closely linked genes usually remain together on the same chromosome after crossing over. Thus, if two genes are closely linked then they will be transmitted together within families.

To better understand linkage it is useful to consider a hypothetical example. If a gene that causes schizophrenia is very close (linked) to a gene that causes eye colour then we would expect schizophrenia and eye colour to be transmitted together in families. If one family had a schizophrenic father with blue eyes and a non-schizophrenic mother with brown eyes then we would expect their schizophrenic children to have blue eyes and their non-schizophrenic children to have brown eyes. This does not mean that eye colour causes schizophrenia but suggests that the genes for eye colour and schizophrenia are close to one another on the human chromosomes. This example is artificial and does not include key details, but it does convey what we mean when we describe two genes as linked to one another.

The potential for finding schizophrenia genes caused much excitement in scientific circles. Indeed, some preliminary findings in the late 1980s and 1990 seemed to indicate that a gene on chromosome 5 played a role in the causation of schizophrenia. Interest in chromosome 5 was motivated by the report of Dr Ann Bassett from Columbia University in 1988 of a single family in which two cases of schizophrenia each had a distinct abnormality of this chromosome. Following this report, Dr Robin Sherrington and colleagues from the University of London studied seven British and Icelandic families having schizophrenic members in at least three generations. Using the new molecular genetic technologies to track the inheritance pattern of schizophrenia in these families, these investigators demonstrated genetic linkage to the part of chromosome 5 that had been implicated by Bassett's report. Taken together, these two findings provided a glimmer of hope that the long search for the genetic cause of schizophrenia was coming to an end. Unfortunately, other linkage studies have not replicated this finding. This same pattern has also been repeatedly observed at dozens of spots throughout the genome, and despite the best efforts of hundreds of scientists working together, it is still difficult to gain consensus on the regions of the genome most likely to harbor schizophrenia-risk genes. Within the last 5 years, several groups working together, including our own, have pooled data to determine where the collective evidence is strongest, and several loci appear to be reliably linked to schizophrenia. These include regions of chromosomes 1, 2q, 3q, 4q, 5q, 8p, and 10q (where 'p' refers to the short arm of the chromosome and 'q' the long arm). Yet, none of these regions has been universally observed to be linked with schizophrenia; it is only when all data are pooled that an overall or average effect suggestive of linkage has been observed.

What can we make of these conflicting results? Some have argued that, if more than one gene can cause schizophrenia then both the positive and the negative findings can be correct. However, as more and more studies fail to find linkage to particular regions, it becomes more reasonable to conclude that the original positive finding may be a false result due to the play of chance. We may not know the truth of this matter for many years since it is possible—some would say very likely—that several genetic subtypes of schizophrenia exist.

This 'false start' in the linkage analysis of schizophrenia has been a sobering experience for many schizophrenia scientists. Although we have a duty to report our findings to the public, we must also be concerned about raising false hopes when the popular press reports findings that cannot be replicated by other investigators.

The problems that have arisen in linkage studies of schizophrenia may indicate that, although advances in medical science have now made it easy to find genes for *simple* single gene disorders, it will be more challenging to find genes for disorders like schizophrenia which appear to have a *complex* mode of inheritance. Scientists studying diseases such as cystic fibrosis and Huntington's disease have shown that it is possible to find genes that cause illness. We call these *simple* single-gene disorders because, when we examine families, we find that the pattern of transmission closely follows the laws of single gene inheritance. In contrast, the mode of inheritance of schizophrenia is unknown and does not conform to the laws of inheritance for single-gene disorders. In such cases, we call the mode of inheritance *complex*.

Association studies

Once regions of certain chromosomes have been implicated from linkage analysis as harboring a risk gene for a disorder, the next step is to identify what specific gene is segregating through families to give rise to that linkage signal. A gene can be selected for such analysis subsequent to linkage analysis as a means to follow-up on evidence for increased genetic similarity at a locus among affected individuals in a family (i.e., a 'positional candidate gene' approach). Alternatively, specific genes can be examined in the absence of linkage information if there is some compelling reason to suspect that the gene influences risk for a given disorder (i.e., a 'functional candidate gene' approach). For example, dopamine-system genes, such as receptors and transporters, are commonly examined as functional candidates for schizophrenia. In contrast to linkage analysis, which uses random DNA markers as proxies for nearby risk genes, genetic association analysis is the appropriate method for determining if a particular gene variant has a direct effect on risk for schizophrenia, or is very tightly linked to such a gene. In the absence of definitive linkage evidence (like the situation we have in schizophrenia), we have now arrived at an era where we can directly test all regions of the genome directly for association with the disorder, using an approach called **genome-wide association scanning**, or GWAS.

If a gene influences the risk for schizophrenia, this should be detectable as an increased frequency of the risk variant of the gene in schizophrenic patients compared to controls who do not have schizophrenia. Within the context of the family, this would be detectable as an increased likelihood of an individual with schizophrenia receiving the risk variant of the gene from his or her parent, even when both the risk and normal variants of the gene were present in the parent and could have been transmitted with equal frequency and likelihood.

In a case-control association study, we simply count the number of each type of variant of a gene that is found in cases and compare these counts with the counts seen in the control group. A simple statistical test can then be used to determine if any genetic variant is more common among schizophrenic patients compared with the control group. If we find such a difference, we refer to the variant that is more common among the patients as the risk variant.

Many genes have been tested for an association with schizophrenia, either because they build proteins thought to be involved in the pathology of the disorder or because they are located in a chromosomal region implicated by linkage analysis. In the former group, several genes have been verified in large pooled samples to have a small but reliable influence on risk for the disorder. Some of these include the genes coding for the serotonin 2A receptor (*HTR2A*) and the dopamine D2 (*DRD2*) and D3 (*DRD3*) receptors. Genes coding for disrupted-in-schizophrenia 1 (*DISC1*), dystrobrevin-binding protein 1 (*DTNBP1*), neuregulin 1 (*NRG1*), and regulator of G-protein signaling 4 (*RGS4*) have emerged as the strongest positional candidate risk genes for schizophrenia, but these findings still require verification.

Aside from these candidate-gene studies, the results of several genome-wide association studies (GWAS) of schizophrenia have started to appear in the literature in the last 5 years. The first of these, reported by Dr Todd Lencz and colleagues, found evidence strongly implicating a cytokine receptor gene (*CSF2RA*) in schizophrenia among a small sample of 178 cases and 144 control subjects. Follow-up sequencing of this gene and its neighbour *IL3RA* (another cytokine receptor subunit) revealed several novel, rare, non-synonymous mutations associated with the disorder. These were among the first schizophrenia-associated variants to emerge from a GWAS; however, they have not been widely replicated, which highlights the continuing frustrations of the genomic era. Despite the strength of evidence, one study is simply not enough to cause us to declare that true schizophrenia-risk genes have been identified. Other genes recently implicated from GWAS of schizophrenia include another common schizophrenia-risk candidate gene, *RELN*, and a novel candidate, *CCDC60*. Fortunately, the early GWAS by Dr Lencz and others have been succeeded by ever-larger studies with ever-improved coverage of the genome and unparalleled ability to resolve genetic signals to small regions of the genome.

A recent collaborative project which pooled the results of several large GWAS has finally identified a small handful of genes that most scientists are willing to declare truly significant. These genes are in the long-implicated *MHC* gene cluster on chromosome 6 and the long-pursued candidate gene *NOTCH4*. The genome-wide significant evidence derived at these loci is highly encouraging, but further work must be done to determine the actual causal genetic variations in the vicinities of these association signals, as the exact polymorphisms evaluated in these studies may not actually have anything to do with risk for the disorder, but instead may simply be markers for the true causal variants in their vicinity. Ironically, the development of technology to perform GWAS, which were intended to simplify and clarify the landscape of genetic risk for schizophrenia, have in fact only shed light on just how complex the human genome is and how a variety of different genetic mechanisms may be operating in this illness. For example, the microarray technologies utilized to detect genetic polymorphisms that are over-represented in people with schizophrenia also have built-in controls that are invariant in all individuals; yet, when scientists evaluated these so-called invariant probes they have seen on repeated occasions that individuals with schizophrenia possessed more or fewer copies of some of these genes than were anticipated. These so-called copy-number variations, or CNVs, are now widely observed to be more prevalent in individuals with the disorder than in those without; however, these are still rare occurrences overall and do not account for the majority of cases of the illness. In addition, the exact regions of the genome that are miscopied in schizophrenia are often different among affected individuals, suggesting that there are again heterogeneous paths from genomic variation to disorder.

Lastly, GWAS have highlighted how much more work needs to be done to understand the contributions of 'rare' or even 'private' mutations in the emergence of schizophrenia. The currently employed GWAS microarray platforms do a very thorough job of providing information on most common variations in the genome and their over- or under-preponderance in affected individuals. From such data, Dr Shaun Purcell and colleagues have estimated that approximately 30% of the risk for schizophrenia can be attributed to about 1000 of these different common variants. Yet, the heritability, or amount of variance in who becomes affected with the disorder that is accounted for by genes overall, is estimated at between 60 and 85%; thus, there is a great deal of 'missing heritability' in schizophrenia not accounted for by common variations. This gives scientists pause, as it suggests the possibility that many cases of schizophrenia may be due to individual or combinations of rare variants that are relatively exclusive to certain families or individuals, and in fact some of these may not have been inherited but acquired de novo during one's lifetime. In the best-case scenario (which we have already ruled out), schizophrenia would be caused by one factor, either genetic or environmental, that would facilitate diagnosis and dictate a treatment avenue. In the worst case scenario, each affected individual has his or her own constellation of risk factors, which makes diagnosis, treatment, and even research much more difficult. We have long assumed that the true scenario lies intermediate to these two extremes, but recent data from GWAS of the disorder have suggested that the answer may lie closer to the more heterogeneous and complex scenario. These leads and others generated from GWAS are now a top research priority and are being vigorously pursued.

Collectively, these studies provide solid support for the suggestion that GWAS of schizophrenia are capable of both identifying genes with significant associations with schizophrenia and potentially broadening the boundaries of existing disease models of the disorder by taking a broad survey of the genome. Yet, as described above, these studies have limitations that may preclude the detection of some association signals or hinder the generalizability of their findings for some time to come. Some of these limitations will be overcome by continued pooling of data to identify the most reliably associated genes; on the other hand, new technologies will also need to be brought to bear on schizophrenia to hasten the rate of risk-gene discovery. Direct DNA sequencing, which 5 years ago could only be accomplished on one individual's genome at a cost of over one million dollars, is very close to entering an era of feasibility for research studies. In fact, even now, the most advanced studies of the disorder are using targeted sequencing approaches, like 'exome sequencing' which covers all protein-coding regions of the genome, to identify risk-associated polymorphisms without the need for imputation or inference due to missing genomic data. Soon, scientists should be able to generate whole-genome data on affected individuals in a reasonable period of time and at a reasonable enough cost to allow the method to be employed on samples large enough to inspire confidence in their results.

Unlike in the past when the application of new genomic technologies was often embraced and touted by scientists with unbridled enthusiasm, today's research is being executed with perhaps a bit more pessimism, or at least caution. Because although we know that having whole-genome data on an affected individual will allow for the strongest conclusions to be drawn, we have become more cognizant of the effects that the environment can have on either facilitating or inhibiting genetic polymorphisms in influencing traits and behaviours. As a general class, we refer to the ways in which the environment can modify the output of the genome as 'epigenetic' effects. Epigenetic modifications are ubiquitous in the human genome, and these factors can have an immense influence on the expression of the genes encoded by the genome. Thus, epigenetic modifications do not change the sequence of the DNA or the type of protein that can be made, but rather these modifications influence how accessible the genome is to the factors that turn it 'on' or 'off', and in so doing can direct how much or how little of a particular protein (or a whole genome's-worth of proteins) can be made. We are now seeing some concrete examples of instances where, for example, genetic polymorphisms that usually increase risk for schizophrenia may be exacerbated or offset depending on the epigenomic modifications present in the vicinity of that gene. We are just beginning to map normal and schizophrenia-associated epigenetic modifications throughout the genome, so it will be some time before we can develop a functional understanding of the impact of epigenetics on schizophrenia; however, we expect that ultimately epigenetics may provide a means for better predicting the risk for the disorder in conjunction with genetic polymorphism data, understanding the ways the environment modifies the risk for schizophrenia, and perhaps designing novel avenues for therapeutic intervention.

The identification of numerous risk genes of varying effect on the liability towards schizophrenia may ultimately make it possible to create a genetic risk profile that will be predictive of future onsets of the disorder. Such a genetic risk profile may also find use in genetic counseling settings to help potential parents understand the risk of schizophrenia to their unborn child and to make decisions based on this information. Most relevant for the treatment of schizophrenia, several genes including *DRD2* and *HTR2A* have also been reported to influence the outcome of medication treatments. As the relationships between these genes and specific aspects of favourable or unfavourable response to medications become further characterized, these too may attain clinical utility in the development and administration of genetically tailored, personalized medication management of schizophrenia. We must emphasize, however, that such uses of genetic data are not possible at this time and may not be possible for some time.

7

How does the environment influence schizophrenia?

➲ Key points

- ◆ Some environmental events contribute to causing schizophrenia, whereas others change the symptoms of schizophrenia in people who have onset with the disorder.

- ◆ The term 'schizophrenogenic' was applied to mothers whose method of upbringing for their child was believed to cause schizophrenia. Research shows that this idea is wrong.

- ◆ Social selection occurs when a geographic region either draws or repulses schizophrenic patients due to the way of life there.

- ◆ The downward drift hypothesis states that people with schizophrenia who cannot perform in a job or function well in daily life will 'drift downward' in class. In support of this hypothesis, researchers found that people with schizophrenia were of a lower socioeconomic class than their parents were at their age.

- ◆ Sporadic cases of schizophrenia are those without a family history of the disease. These patients are more likely to have brain abnormalities or atrophy, and these cases are more likely to have had birth complications.

- ◆ Stressful life events are often present at the onset of schizophrenic symptoms.

Although the evidence for a genetic contribution to the transmission of schizophrenia is very strong, the lack of complete concordance between identical twins suggests that environmental events also play a role in causing schizophrenia. We define an 'environmental risk factor' as any event that is not due to the genes carried by the father's sperm and the mother's egg before conception. These events may be biological (e.g., head injuries, viral infections), psychological (e.g., disrupted family relationships), or social (e.g., poverty).

Over the past several decades, researchers have produced evidence implicating environmental risk factors in at least some cases of schizophrenia. Before reviewing this research we must make a crucial distinction: some environmental factors may *cause* schizophrenia whereas others *modify* the illness in someone who is already sick. In this book we use the term 'cause' to refer to any agent that can produce the illness in someone who is not and has never been ill with schizophrenia. This cause does not have to be either necessary or sufficient. This means that other causes may exist that also produce the illness and that the putative cause may require the presence of another cause for the illness to be expressed. We use the term 'modifier' to refer to anything that changes the symptoms of the illness in someone who is already sick. As we discuss in a subsequent chapter, knowledge of modifiers can help with the treatment of the disorder. However, they should not be confused with causes.

Do environmental risk factors cause schizophrenia?

Scientists who study schizophrenia and other psychiatric disorders have long abandoned the 'nature–nurture' controversy. In times past, many philosophers and scientists had taken one of two extreme positions. Some believed that psychiatric illness was exclusively caused by innate, genetic factors; others posited that mental disease was the sole product of adverse environmental events. Today, we realize that useful scientific solutions are not forthcoming from the simplistic question 'What causes schizophrenia: genes or environment?' As Dr Paul Meehl observed several decades ago, the appropriate question is much more complicated: 'What group of environmental risk factors work together with what genes to produce schizophrenia?'

Before discussing specific environmental risk factors that may cause schizophrenia we should clarify why we believe that the study of such factors is essential. First, twin studies of schizophrenia show that the genetically identical co-twins of people with schizophrenia develop schizophrenia only 50% of the time. This is remarkable. When the co-twin of a schizophrenic person does not also have schizophrenia, this means that the schizophrenia risk genes require an environmental event to trigger the genetic risk for the disorder. Twin studies show that, without a doubt, people can carry schizophrenia-risk genes without ever getting sick with the illness. This provides a strong rationale for the study of environmental events.

A second reason to study environmental risk factors is that they may be amenable to change and could therefore be useful for treatment planning. Many environmental factors can be modified. For example, if specific diets or bad parenting caused schizophrenia, then public programs or family therapies could be established with the goal of preventing the illness. The eventual creation of such treatments is often the long-term goal of scientists who study environmental risk factors.

Family relationships

For the first two-thirds of the twentieth century, the mental health professions were dominated by theorists, researchers, and clinicians who believed that most mental illness was caused by events that interrupted, delayed, or otherwise disrupted psychological development. Since the family environment strongly influences psychological well-being, it seemed reasonable to focus on family relationships as a potential cause of schizophrenia. Thus, theories positing that families caused schizophrenia emerged from observations made by clinicians and researchers.

Unfortunately, many of these theories were offered as fact even though no scientific data had been generated to back them up. We hope in this chapter to show the advantage of rigorous scientific research over myths, old wives' tales, and misunderstandings based on speculation and opinion rather than fact. We shall start by discussing some hypotheses that have now been discredited. It is sad to say that, before these theories had been shown to be false, many relatives, especially mothers, of people with schizophrenia had been told that their method of child-rearing caused the illness. This was a terrible burden to bear. We can only hope that most of these people have since learned the truth about these theories.

Schizophrenogenic mothers

At one time, many mental health clinicians and researchers believed that personality traits of mothers caused schizophrenia in their children. These mothers were labeled 'schizophrenogenic' to indicate that they caused schizophrenia. The rationale for this theory was the belief—not fact—that mothers of schizophrenic patients tended to be over-protective, hostile, and unable to understand their children's feelings. These abnormal attitudes were thought to *create* schizophrenic behaviour in their children.

However, this argument did not take into account the possibility that the mother's attitudes might develop *as a consequence* of having a child with schizophrenia. Even if it could be shown that the mother had such traits before the onset of her child's schizophrenia, it is possible that unusual characteristics of the pre-schizophrenic child might have brought out such attitudes. There is also another possibility. The mothers of individuals with schizophrenia may have passed schizophrenia susceptibility genes to their schizophrenic child. Recall that many people who carry genetic risk factors for schizophrenia will not develop schizo-phrenia. They may have a personality disorder or may be completely normal. It is possible that the genetic contributors to schizophrenia may be expressed in traits such as over-protectiveness or hostility. Thus, any so-called schizophreno-genic traits might also be caused by the genetic causes of schizophrenia. We do not know why many clinicians embraced the theory of the schizophrenogenic mother, but studies have shown that the way in which mothers (or fathers) rear their children does not cause (or prevent) schizophrenia.

Double-bind theory

Mothers or mothers-to-be reading this book may wonder whether fathers of schizophrenic patients have also been studied. If the parent–child relationship is important, then surely the father's personality should also be considered. And, in fact, fathers were included in another theory that implicated a particular type of abnormal communication, which could involve the mother or the father. In this 'double-bind' communication, the child is repeatedly exposed to contradictory messages. For example, the parent might tell the child that she may go out but, at the same time, forbid her to do so with a contradictory gesture. The parent's verbal message requires one response, whereas that parent's deeper message requires the opposite.

The double-bind theory of schizophrenia appeared to explain some of the behaviour of people with schizophrenia. Such communication had the poten-tial to make them withdraw into a fantasy world. Also, it seemed to encourage, if not teach, irrational behaviour. However, the double-bind theory grew out of a small number of clinical observations of the relationship between people with schizophrenia and their parents. At first sight both logical and plausible, it was widely applied to the treatment of schizophrenia, until conclusive evi-dence from well-designed experiments made it suspect. Today, it is no longer commonly believed and applied in the treatment of schizophrenia.

Parents' marital relationship

Another hypothesis focused on the possibility that an abnormal relationship between mothers and fathers caused schizophrenia in their children. The basic idea here was that children observing the inappropriate behaviour of their parents would learn to respond with irrational, psychotic behaviour. Two kinds of abnormal marital relationships were characterized. The first was called the 'skewed' relationship. This occurred when one parent yielded to the abnormal parent who then dominated the family. This relationship was thought to be commonly found among parents of male schizophrenic patients. The mother tended to be dominant and the father passive. Consequently the mother, unable to find emotional satisfaction from the father, turned to her son instead.

The other abnormal marital relationship was called 'marital schism'. In these relationships the parents were in chronic conflict. Each ignored their mutual needs to pursue their own separate goals. In the process, each competed for the child's support. Proponents of this hypothesis said that marital schism was common between the parents of female schizophrenic patients.

The ideas of marital skew and marital schism originated from interviews with a small number of families having a child with schizophrenia. However, subsequent studies have shown that these two abnormal marital relationships are also found in families not having schizophrenic children. There is no reason to believe that such relationships are specific to the parents of individuals with schizophrenia. Thus, we can conclude that abnormal parental marital relationships do not cause schizophrenia.

Disordered family communication

About 30 years ago, a study at the US National Institute of Mental Health set out to determine if disordered family communication caused schizophrenia. In a series of controlled experiments, patterns of family interaction were studied, using taped interviews and psychological tests. The results, based on intensive studies of four families each having a child with schizophrenia, revealed that parents of schizophrenics displayed two types of disordered communication: the first was 'amorphous' thinking. It consisted of vague ideas without clear thinking. The second was 'fragmented' thinking, which described thoughts that were disjointed from one another. Here, the basic ideas expressed by the parents were clear but the links between ideas were weak.

These two styles of communication were not restricted to one parent but were assumed to be characteristics of the family as a whole. The researchers theorized that these types of communication deviance influenced the cognitive development of the children. Consequently, the various kinds of schizophrenic thought disorder were said to be a direct result of 'amorphous' and 'fragmented' family communications.

To test this hypothesis, researchers tested three parent groups based on the diagnosis of their child as having schizophrenia, neurosis (relatively minor mental illness), or no mental disorder. Seventy-eight per cent of the parental pairs were classified correctly according to the diagnostic group of their children. It was found that the fathers of schizophrenic patients were more likely to be abnormal than the fathers of neurotic patients or normal controls; but no such difference was found between the mothers of schizophrenic and neurotic patients.

An attempt to reproduce these findings at the University of London's Institute of Psychiatry produced different results. Using the same scoring system, the British investigators compared the parents of schizophrenic and of neurotic patients. Although this study reproduced the finding with regard to the fathers, the characteristic differences between the fathers of schizophrenic patients and of neurotics were less impressive than in the American study. This was probably because the British and American samples differed in their definitions of schizophrenia. In fact, whereas the British patients had positive schizophrenic symptoms of delusions and hallucinations, the American patients had more negative symptoms along with evidence of chronic personality disorganization.

It is possible that a genetic component in the style of communication may have affected the outcome. As stressed before, the interaction of heredity and environment cannot be ignored in any family study; it is still uncertain whether disordered family communication is specific to schizophrenia or whether it could be found in a wide variety of mental illnesses. It is also likely that any abnormal communication observed among the parents is influenced by the same genes that confer risk for schizophrenia itself. Many of these parents may have had schizotypal personality disorder or other, mild manifestations of schizophrenia genes. However, if there is a causal relationship between abnormal communication and schizophrenia in offspring, improvements in family communication should prevent schizophrenia. We know of no concrete evidence supporting this prediction.

Children at risk for schizophrenia

Most of the family studies described so far were based on observations made after the affected individuals developed schizophrenia. Unfortunately, it is often difficult for patients and their families to remember accurately events that took place before the onset of schizophrenia. Another possible source of inaccuracy exists in these studies: abnormal characteristics in the parents could represent the response of the parents to the schizophrenic behaviour of their children. To eliminate these shortcomings, a group of children would have to be studied from birth to the time when some of them develop schizophrenia, recording all the characteristics of the children and the families. When one of the children in the study develops schizophrenia, the noteworthy characteristics of his family could be identified.

The lifetime risk for schizophrenia is about 1%. Thus, if 100 children were selected at birth for such a study, only one of them would have schizophrenia after 40 years of observations. In order to obtain 100 individuals with schizophrenia for study, we would need to follow 10,000 children from birth to the age of 40. Such a study, though ideal, is clearly impractical. One way to reduce the number of children for the study would be to select children with a high risk of developing schizophrenia. The best way to create such a sample is to study children having schizophrenic parents. Since the lifetime risk of schizophrenia is about ten times higher in such children, the number of children under observation could be reduced by one-tenth. This strategy has been used to study biological aspects of schizophrenia, but is unsuitable for the study of parental attitudes and family interaction because the selected children are already genetically predisposed to schizophrenia. It is therefore very difficult to separate the environmental and genetic components. And although the size of the sample can be reduced by studying only high-risk children and their families, the need for long-term follow-up makes such studies very time-consuming and expensive. It is sometimes possible, however, to use existing records from child guidance clinics and schools.

Studies based on such records, written long before the onset of schizophrenia, have shown that the parents of schizophrenic patients, particularly mothers, have more often been in conflict with their children, and demonstrated more signs of over-concern and protectiveness, than the parents of normal children. These parental abnormalities, however, cannot be regarded as evidence for an exclusively psychosocial theory of the cause of schizophrenia, unless genetic influences and the psychological reaction of the parents to the child's abnormal behaviour before the onset of schizophrenia can be ruled out. Studies of adoptive parents of schizophrenic patients have been designed specifically to separate the environmental and genetic influences of parental abnormalities on their schizophrenic children. As we reviewed earlier, adoption studies have found that schizophrenia is due more to genetic than to environmental transmission; no convincing evidence exists to support a direct link between parental rearing factors and the development of schizophrenia. On the contrary, adoption study evidence suggests that there is no causal relationship between rearing factors and schizophrenia.

Most notably, adoption studies have found an increased risk for schizophrenia among children born to schizophrenic mothers and raised by persons without a past history of psychiatric disorder. On the other hand, children born to non-mentally ill parents but raised by adoptive parents with severe mental illness did not show an increased rate for schizophrenic disorders. These studies strongly indicate that rearing factors are not crucial to the development of schizophrenia.

Social environment

The epidemiological studies we discussed in previous chapters show that schizophrenia occurs around the world. It is not limited by geographic region, political system, economic system, or culture. However, the frequency of schizophrenia varies according to sociocultural background. Two extremes of the prevalence rate for schizophrenia were reported from a small community in northern Sweden on the one hand, and the Hutterites of North America on the other: the prevalence was 10.8 per 1000 in the former and 1.1 per 1000 in the latter. Such differences in prevalence between cultures led some researchers to hypothesize that sociocultural aspects of the environment might cause schizophrenia. In contrast, others argued that these differences were due to **social selection**. Social selection occurs when sociocultural characteristics of a region make it more or less likely that the mentally ill will move to or away from it. When this occurs, the culture of the community does not cause the illness, it merely makes it more or less likely that the patient will want to, or is able to, live there.

The Hutterites are a North American Anabaptist religious sect. They live austere and pious lives in a close-knit farming community. The probable explanation for the low prevalence of schizophrenia among the Hutterites is that those with schizophrenic traits would have moved out of such communities due to the high levels of social interaction expected by their peers. In north Sweden, the lifetime risk of schizophrenia was three times as high as in other Scandinavian areas. The climate in north Sweden is severe and the people live extremely isolated lives. Such an environment might be appealing to individuals with schizophrenia. Also, people who do not have schizophrenia may not tolerate such extreme social isolation. They would tend to move away, leaving behind those who were genetically predisposed to schizophrenia and more tolerant of extreme social isolation. A high frequency of cousin marriages was also found in this isolated area; such marriages within a population which already carried genes for schizophrenia would have further increased the high risk rate of schizophrenia in this community.

Socioeconomic status

Epidemiological studies have taken a careful look at the relationship between socioeconomic status and mental illness. People living in the lower social classes are subjected to many disadvantages. Poverty, malnutrition, poor prenatal care of mothers, poor medical care, and chaotic family situations are a few examples of circumstances that could adversely affect mental health. Clearly, it is reasonable to suggest that such factors will have a negative impact on the development of children, leading to an increased risk for schizophrenia.

Researchers were not surprised when they found higher admission rates for schizophrenia among inner-city, low social-class dwellers, in both Europe and America. On the basis of this finding, some concluded that the social disorganization, economic deprivation, poor health, and limited educational opportunities among inner-city dwellers caused schizophrenia in predisposed persons. This raised a key question: 'Does low social class cause schizophrenia or does schizophrenia cause low social class?' It soon became apparent that the second proposed direction of causation was as reasonable as the first. As we have described in previous chapters, schizophrenia leads to massive changes in perceptions, thinking, and social behaviour. Since many patients cannot function well in school or in a job, they can 'drift downward' to the lower social classes. So, again, researchers faced the question of social causation versus social selection.

To examine the **downward drift** hypothesis, epidemiologists tested a simple proposition. If downward drift did not occur, then individuals with schizophrenia should have the same socioeconomic status that their parents did at the same age. However, studies showed that individuals with schizophrenia were more likely than controls to have a lower social status than their parents. Also, studies found that the fathers of individuals with schizophrenia did not differ in social class from the fathers of people without schizophrenia. Thus, individuals with schizophrenia are not exposed to the adversities of lower-class life more than non-schizophrenic individuals.

A study by Dr Bruce Dohrenwend provided additional evidence that low social class does not cause schizophrenia. Dr Dohrenwend and colleagues noted that the study of disadvantaged ethnic groups could clarify this issue because, to some extent, their presence in the lower social classes is due to discrimination, not to lack of ability to achieve. He reasoned that if social adversity caused schizophrenia, then, since discrimination is a form of social adversity, minorities should be at *greater* risk for schizophrenia compared with non-minorities. Moreover, this increased risk for schizophrenia should be evident in all social classes. In contrast, if schizophrenia causes a downward drift in social class, then in the lower social classes, minorities should have a *lower* risk for schizophrenia. This prediction is based on the following reasoning. Because of discrimination many members of minority groups who are psychiatrically healthy and capable of achievement will not move up in social class. If this is true, then their presence in the lower social classes should *decrease* the rate of schizophrenia in lower class minorities. In contrast, since schizophrenic members of non-minority groups would drift downward, this should *increase* the rate of schizophrenia in non-minority persons in the lower classes.

The results of this study supported the downward drift hypothesis. Most notable in this regard was the risk for schizophrenia among lower-class men. This risk was 4% among the ethnically advantaged and 2% among the disadvantaged.

These findings, taken together with previous studies, suggest that schizophrenia causes patients to have a lower social class than they would have if they had not become ill. This is consistent with the fact that schizophrenia makes it very difficult for patients to deal effectively in social or occupational situations. Their social and occupational impairments make it likely that they will not achieve the high levels of economic and educational success required to move out of the lower social strata. Therefore, we and others have concluded that low socioeconomic status is a consequence, rather than a cause, of schizophrenia.

Schizophrenia as a symptom of sick society

A minority of mental health professionals argue that schizophrenia is symptomatic of a sick society. From this viewpoint schizophrenia is a means of coping with the unreasonable social forces exerted upon the patient. This social theory does not posit that low social class causes schizophrenia but rather that all social classes are at risk for the illness.

Surprisingly, the advocates of this hypothesis claim that the schizophrenic process is a 'therapeutic experience'; the goal of therapy is to help guide the patient through this experience, not to stop it. These therapists believe that the pressures of our ailing society are exerted through the family and that one member of the family is singled out to bear the burden. 'Schizophrenia' is thought of as a label attached to this person as a result of the social process. Extreme followers of this theory regard the individual with schizophrenia as a person struggling to achieve autonomy from the demands of his parents; by becoming schizophrenic, he actually achieves his autonomy.

Since the psychotic symptoms of schizophrenia are seen as helpful to the patient, any treatment designed to cut short episodes of schizophrenia is, accordingly, thought to be anti-therapeutic. Since the disturbed family relationship is the source of schizophrenic symptoms, treatment should not only involve the family, but also aim at establishing a special kind of corrective relationship between patient and therapist. Although this view of schizophrenia is accepted by some lay and professional workers, the assumptions on which it is based have not survived critical, scientific examination.

Biological environmental risk factors

During the past four decades, scientists have moved away from studying family relationships and the social environment as primary causes of schizophrenia.

Indeed, the failure of such theories to withstand the rigors of scientific testing has led many to study environmental events that have biological significance for the developing human brain. At this point, the reader must understand that these events are called 'biological' as opposed to 'psychological' or 'social' because they are known to disturb biological functioning. Thus, we refer to factors such as social class and family relationships as non-biological because their implications for biological functioning are unclear. In contrast, it is relatively easy to see how physical events like head injury or viral infection lead to brain damage. The biological implications of these latter events are straightforward. Thus, the distinction between biological and non-biological factors actually reflects our state of knowledge (or lack of it) regarding how events impinge on human biology. We can easily envision some day when the biological implications of psychological and social stresses are so well understood that the distinction we draw today between biological and non-biological events will no longer be needed.

Pregnancy and delivery complications

Any event that affects the fetus in the mother's uterus before birth is classified as a prenatal event. These include physical trauma, malnutrition, infection, and intoxication. Perinatal events are those that occur at the time of birth. Examples are physical injury, lack of oxygen, infection, and bleeding. Events occurring after birth, whether biological or psychosocial, are called postnatal. When postnatal events occur close to the time of birth they are included with pre- and perinatal events under the term 'pregnancy and delivery complications', or **PDCs** for short.

Many studies have found increased rates of PDCs in the births of children who eventually develop schizophrenia. For example, individuals with schizophrenia are more likely to have been born prematurely and to have had relatively low birth weights. Other types of PDCs have also been found. What has puzzled researchers is that the association between PDCs and schizophrenia is not strong. Although individuals with schizophrenia are more likely to have had PDCs, these were fairly common in the general population. As a result, the great majority of babies who experienced the PDCs did not develop schizophrenia.

When researchers considered the PDC study results in combination with those of genetic studies, a simple, yet powerful hypothesis emerged. It appeared likely that the effect of PDCs was to activate the genetic predisposition to schizophrenia. They reasoned that the individual with schizophrenia inherits a liability or predisposition to develop schizophrenia. However, an environmental event is needed to trigger the predisposition. This is sometimes called the 'diathesis–stress' theory of schizophrenia because it requires both a genetic predisposition (diathesis) and an adverse environmental event (stress) for an individual to develop schizophrenia.

Dr Sarnoff Mednick found strong support for the diathesis–stress theory in a study of children born to mothers with schizophrenia. This study first showed that these 'high–risk' children were not more likely than other children to have PDCs. Thus, the presence of schizophrenia in the mother does not predict a more complicated birth for the child. This means that the genetic predisposition (having a schizophrenic mother) is not confounded with the environmental stress (the PDCs). Dr Mednick and colleagues found that, among the high–risk children, PDCs were predictive of subsequent psychiatric abnormality, including schizophrenia. They also found that those children with the least complicated births were more likely to have 'borderline schizophrenia'. This refers to a syndrome that resembles schizophrenia in a very mild form. In today's diagnostic language we would say that they have schizotypal personality disorder. Overall, the results of this series of studies suggested that children with the genetic predisposition to schizophrenia would develop schizophrenia if they had PDCs.

The findings of Dr Mednick's group are intriguing, but, like many findings in schizophrenia, the final truth is likely to be more complex. There is general agreement that PDCs are predictive of subsequent schizophrenia and of measurable brain abnormalities. Thus, it seems clear that PDCs have a certain biological impact. However, not all family studies support the idea that PDCs interact with a genetic predisposition to produce schizophrenia. Others have raised the possibility that PDCs cause a non–genetic form of schizophrenia. This alternative theory suggests that PDCs can cause schizophrenia in people who do not have the genetic predisposition. In support of this, several studies found more PDCs among patients without a family history of schizophrenia compared with patients with a family history. However, other studies find no difference. These findings highlight the complexity of the causal chain of events leading to schizophrenia. It seems likely that PDCs either add to the causal effects of genes or trigger these effects. In rare cases they may act alone to cause a non-genetic form of schizophrenia.

The viral hypothesis

Most of us are familiar with viruses. These creatures, which cannot be seen without specialized microscopes, have made all of us ill at one time or another with mild colds, the flu, or gastrointestinal problems. We also know, from the epidemic caused by the AIDS virus, that viruses can be extremely dangerous. This tells us that viruses can have a wide range of effects, from mild discomfort to death. Thus, the reader will not be surprised about speculation that a virus might cause schizophrenia.

The viral hypothesis of schizophrenia has impressed many scientists as a reasonable way of explaining several epidemiological and clinical observations. Foremost among these is the finding that the births of individuals with schizophrenia are more likely to occur during the late winter and spring months than during other times of the year. Children born during these months are at increased risk for exposure to viruses while they are in the womb. Researchers reasoned that the effects of a virus at such an early age might alter the development of the brain in an abnormal direction. This 'season of birth effect' motivated the idea that a virus, toxic to the human brain, might be involved in the aetiology of some cases of schizophrenia. Interestingly, some studies found that the season of birth effect was strongest among patients without a family history of schizophrenia. Thus, it may be that viral cases of schizophrenia do not have a genetic origin, or that genetic factors are of lesser importance in such cases.

Although the season of birth effect is the most compelling evidence in favour of a viral cause of schizophrenia, other facts are also consistent with this theory. First, if a virus attacking the developing brain of a fetus causes schizophrenia, we would expect to observe additional evidence of such effects. Two such effects have been observed in schizophrenia. First, individuals with schizophrenia have elevated rates of physical anomalies. These are unusual characteristics in the shape of body parts. For example, facial deformities would be considered physical anomalies. Since physical anomalies can be caused by viruses that attack the fetus, the high rate of anomalies among individuals with schizophrenia supports the viral hypothesis. Second, some individuals with schizophrenia have unusual fingerprints. Although both physical anomalies and unusual fingerprints could be caused by PDCs or genetic abnormalities, their presence in schizophrenia could be the calling card from a viral attack on the brain.

The viral theory of schizophrenia has also been tested in studies of persons born during influenza epidemics. Since the influenza virus can create defects in the brain, fetuses exposed to the virus should have an increased risk for schizophrenia. One study examined adults in Finland who had been fetuses during a 1957 epidemic of influenza. Those adults who had been exposed to the epidemic during months 4, 5, or 6 of their mothers' pregnancy were at increased risk for subsequently being diagnosed with schizophrenia. This strongly suggests that the influenza virus caused schizophrenia in some people. However, a Scottish study failed to consistently find an increased risk for schizophrenia associated with influenza epidemics in 1918, 1919, or 1957, and only limited evidence of an association between viral epidemics and schizophrenia was found in an American study. Although the Finnish results were supported in a Danish sample, more research is needed to definitively conclude that viral infection during fetal development causes schizophrenia.

Studies of 'familial' and 'sporadic' schizophrenia

As we have alluded to above, some studies of biological environmental factors have concluded that cases of 'sporadic' schizophrenia may exist. The word **sporadic** refers to cases that do not have a familial origin. Hence, the illness occurs only rarely (sporadically) within a given family. In contrast, **familial** schizophrenia refers to cases of the illness that co-occur with other cases in the same family. We, and others, use the word 'familial' instead of 'genetic' because an illness may cluster in families for non-genetic reasons. Nevertheless, we believe that most cases of familial schizophrenia are indeed of a genetic origin, or have some genetic contribution.

The familial/sporadic point of view is an alternative to the diathesis–stress theory discussed above. The basic idea here is that schizophrenia may be caused by either genetic or environmental factors. For example, one type of schizophrenia might be due to a single gene or (more likely) a group of risk genes, but another could be caused by a virus. This may explain why it has been so difficult for researchers to definitively find a single cause for the disease. At our current stage of knowledge there is no infallible method for distinguishing between genetic and non-genetic forms of the illness. However, we can classify patients as either familial or sporadic. Patients having one or more relatives with schizophrenia are called familial. Those with no ill relatives are designated as sporadic. Of course, the categories familial and sporadic are not perfect indicators of the genetic and non-genetic categories, as they are based on self-report and limited knowledge of the ancestral pattern of illness. However, from any differences between familial and sporadic cases we may reasonably infer sources of genetic and environmental causation.

Familial and sporadic individuals with schizophrenia do not differ with regard to demographic measures such as age and sex. They also tend to be similar with respect to clinical aspects of the illness, such as symptoms, age at onset, and need for hospitalization. In contrast, there are differences in measures of brain functioning. Most notably, difficulties sustaining attention are more common among familial schizophrenic patients. These patients find it difficult to perform tasks that require them to focus on an object for long periods of time. In other words, they are distractible; their attention is easily diverted to other aspects of the world around them. Patients with sporadic schizophrenia are more likely to have structural brain abnormalities when they are examined with methods like **computerized axial tomography (CAT) scans** or **magnetic resonance imaging (MRI)** that take pictures of brain structures. The abnormalities we refer to here indicate that the brains of sporadic patients show evidence of atrophy or loss of brain cells. Also, pregnancy and delivery complications and winter births tend to be more common among sporadic cases of schizophrenia compared with familial cases. We cannot draw strong conclusions from these studies because, although most studies support these findings, some do not. Nevertheless, the available results fit well with the idea that adverse environmental events can adversely impact neurodevelopment which leads to a non-genetic form of schizophrenia.

Another approach for identifying patients with possible genetic and environmental forms of an illness requires the comparison of concordant and discordant monozygotic (MZ) twins. If twins are monozygotic then their genes are identical. Thus, if a trait is completely determined by genetic factors both twins should express it. Given these facts, MZ twin pairs that are concordant for schizophrenia are more likely to have a genetic form of schizophrenia. In contrast, MZ pairs discordant for the illness might possibly have an environmental form of schizophrenia. Researchers at the Maudsley Hospital in London, England, examined 21 MZ pairs; 9 were concordant for schizophrenia and 12 were discordant. There were no differences in measures of structural brain abnormalities between the schizophrenic members of discordant and concordant pairs. However, those without a family history of schizophrenia had more brain atrophy. These researchers also found more pregnancy and delivery complications among the individuals with schizophrenia who belonged to the discordant MZ pairs.

If twins are discordant because of a non-genetic cause of schizophrenia, then only the relatives of concordant pairs should be at increased risk for the illness. While some studies find this result, others do not. These studies indicate that some of the twins in discordant pairs have a genetic illness. How large the sporadic subset might be is not known.

In summary, studies of familial and sporadic individuals with schizophrenia have produced mixed results. Some are consistent with the idea that there are non-genetic forms of schizophrenia. It seems likely that pregnancy and delivery complications and the actions of a virus are responsible for some of these apparently non-genetic cases. These studies cannot rule out the diathesis–stress model of schizophrenia discussed earlier. In fact, some of these studies are more consistent with this theory than they are with the proposition that some non-genetic forms exist. Clearly, more research is needed to choose between these two ideas or to determine which cases of schizophrenia are due to each type of cause.

8

Is schizophrenia a brain disorder?

➜ Key points

♦ Neuroimaging studies have found brain atrophy in 20–50% of people with schizophrenia.

♦ People with schizophrenia have reduced metabolic activity in some parts of the brain, suggesting that the schizophrenic brain cannot react to stimuli quickly or as effectively as a normal brain.

♦ Blood flow to the frontal cortex is decreased in schizophrenic patients, who also perform poorly on tests of attention, motor function, and abstraction—all of which are functions of the frontal cortex.

♦ People with schizophrenia have greater left-brain dysfunction (as measured by language and writing tasks) than right-brain dysfunction (as measured by spatial tasks).

♦ The dopamine theory states that schizophrenia is caused by overactivity of a brain chemical called dopamine. While this theory is overly simplistic, much data have accumulated to suggest that having too much dopamine is probably one of the brain defects leading to schizophrenia.

In the language of psychiatry, disorders that alter the functioning of psychological or emotional processes are classified as either 'symptomatic' or 'idiopathic'. Symptomatic disorders are those for which there is a known physical cause. For example, temporal lobe epilepsy, strokes, and brain tumours can lead to disturbed mental functioning and emotional expression. In these cases the physical cause can be demonstrated by using electroencephalograms (which measure the electrical activity of the brain), X-rays, or similar, but more sophisticated, methods of assessment. In contrast, we say a disorder is idiopathic if it has no *known* physical cause. We emphasize the word 'known' because most scientists expect that a physical cause of schizophrenia will someday be discovered. The term 'idiopathic' originally reflected the belief that these disorders were due to psychological and social events that had no physical effects on the brain.

When the first edition of this book was published, psychiatry was undergoing a revolution in its approach to mental illness, especially schizophrenia. Many scientists and clinicians were beginning to question the belief that schizophrenia was rooted in psychological and family conflict. Instead, they surmised that the massive alterations in thought and emotion afflicting the individual with schizophrenia were due to a disease of the brain.

In this chapter we review evidence showing that biological processes are disrupted in the brains of individuals with schizophrenia. During the past century, scientists have created many methods for studying the brain. As each of these new neurodiagnostic technologies emerged, they were swiftly applied to the study of schizophrenia. As we shall see, most of these measurements led to the same conclusion: namely, that the structure and function of the brains of some individuals with schizophrenia were not normal. We are, however, still uncertain about many of the details of the **aetiology** and **pathophysiology** of the disorder. Aetiology refers to the causes of brain dysfunction (e.g., defective genes, environmental risk factors); pathophysiology denotes the specific modifications of the brain that lead to illness (e.g., brain atrophy, too much dopamine). For example, a mutation in a gene controlling brain cell physiology might be the aetiology of schizophrenia. The corresponding pathophysiology might be atrophy of the brain as measured by a brain scan.

Structural brain abnormalities

We use the phrase 'structural brain abnormalities' to refer to any unusual changes in the form or configuration of the brain observed in individuals with schizophrenia but not in healthy people. The most direct way to observe such changes is to literally look at the brain, after death, using methods from neuropathology. Many such studies have been done thanks to the generosity of individuals who agreed to donate their brain to research following their death. We can draw two major conclusions from the results of these neuropathological studies of schizophrenia. First, abnormalities of the brain are common among individuals with schizophrenia. Second, researchers have not found a single abnormality that is found in all or even most brains from individuals with schizophrenia. This is a curious result, which we will see mirrored by other methods of studying the schizophrenic brain. Whereas most well-defined brain diseases leave a distinct pathophysiological 'signature' on the brain, this is not the case for schizophrenia.

Neuropathology studies are difficult to do because we must wait for the patient's death before examining the brain. Fortunately, there are several methods that allow us to study the structure of the brain in living patients. Collectively, these methods are called 'imaging' techniques because they provide us with an image of the living brain. They are similar to the simple X-ray procedure that most of us have experienced in our doctor's office. Like the X-ray, these imaging methods create a picture of the brain that can be used to find abnormalities.

Structural abnormalities have been found in a veritable plethora of cortical and subcortical brain structures in people with schizophrenia, from postmortem tissue analysis and from structural brain imaging techniques such as computer-assisted tomography and magnetic resonance imaging (MRI) scans. An emerging consensus is identifying those brain structures that have been most consistently implicated as disrupted in schizophrenia. Increased lateral ventricular volume is frequently observed, as well as volumetric decreases in the dorsolateral and medial prefrontal cortices, cingulate and paracingulate cortices, hippocampus, parahippocampal and superior temporal gyri, septum pellucidum, and thalamus. These abnormalities of brain structure may be core features of the disorder or, at the very least, are among the most prevalent and/or most severe structural brain abnormalities among schizophrenic patients.

In 1927, a then new method known as 'pneumonoencephalography' found that 18 of 19 individuals with schizophrenia had enlarged ventricles. Ventricles are spaces within the brain containing fluid, but not solid brain substance. Ventricles enlarge when the brain substance that surrounds them loses brain cells. We refer to this loss of brain cells as 'atrophy'. Thus, patients with larger ventricles have fewer brain cells. This early finding was confirmed in subsequent pneumonoencephalographic studies. Unfortunately, these pioneering findings were largely ignored since psychological theories of schizophrenia were in vogue.

Psychiatry rediscovered brain atrophy in schizophrenia in 1976 when Drs Eva Johnstone and Timothy Crow and colleagues of the British Medical Research Council Clinical Research Center reported ventricular enlargement in patients with schizophrenia evaluated with the imaging method known as computerized axial tomography (CAT). The CAT scanner takes pictures of the living brain in small 'slices'. This allowed researchers to visualize the inner portions of the brain in a more accurate manner than had been previously possible. In the 1980s the method of MRI was also applied to schizophrenia. MRI scans provide a three-dimensional image of the living brain in a manner that allows us to see more of the details of brain structure than had been possible with the CAT scan. Many CAT scan and MRI scan studies of schizophrenia confirmed that some patients with schizophrenia have larger than normal ventricles. In fact, a 2010 review of longitudinal structural neuroimaging studies has also shown that ventricular enlargement in schizophrenia is progressive over the course of many years, which challenges a strictly neurodevelopmental view of the disorder. In addition to confirming the finding of ventricular enlargement, several MRI studies report reduced brain tissue volumes in specific regions of the schizophrenic brain. For example, a 2005 review of all structural MRI studies of schizophrenia found that as many as 50 discrete brain regions showed some grey or white matter volumetric deficit in patients with schizophrenia, relative to healthy comparison subjects. The brain regions found most consistently to be abnormally structured in schizophrenia included the left superior temporal gyrus and the left medial temporal lobe.

More work is needed to pinpoint all regions of tissue loss in the brain and to determine the significance of large ventricles for people with schizophrenia. Several difficulties are evident. Although, as a group, individuals with schizophrenia have larger ventricles than normal, many individuals with schizophrenia have normal ventricles. Depending on the group of patients studied, only 20–50% of individuals with schizophrenia will have enlarged ventricles. However, when it does occur, the ventricular enlargement associated with schizophrenia is present at the onset of the illness. Thus, it is not a side effect of chronic hospitalization, drug treatment, or other factors associated with schizophrenia.

Patients with enlarged ventricles differ from other patients in several ways. They tend to have more negative symptoms such as flatness of affect and social withdrawal. They are also more likely to have difficulties thinking, as measured by neuropsychological tests. In many ways their illness appears to be more severe. They usually cannot live alone but require either permanent hospitalization or the structure of a halfway house or foster home. When they are hospitalized they require relatively long hospital stays and do not respond well to most treatment programs. Also, as noted in a previous chapter, ventricular enlargement is more common among individuals with schizophrenia without a family history of schizophrenia. These results initially suggested that enlarged ventricles might identify a subtype of schizophrenia. However, researchers have not yet been able to isolate a homogeneous subtype with this feature. Moreover, ventricular enlargement is not limited to schizophrenia. It has also been reported in other psychiatric disorders including bipolar disorder, schizoaffective disorder, and obsessive-compulsive disorder.

The integrity of brain structure in schizoaffective disorder has not received much research attention independent from schizophrenia; rather, patients with schizoaffective disorder are usually examined jointly with individuals with schizophrenia, reflecting the close proximity of the former to the latter on the continuum of clinical features and (presumed) aetiology. Yet, the limited number of studies that have investigated the state of the brain in schizoaffective disorder have provided only mixed evidence for common morphology in the two disorders and, in fact, have not noted many structural deficits. For example, features sometimes seen in individuals with schizophrenia (such as striatal enlargement and cerebral volume reductions) have each only been noted in one of three existing studies of schizoaffective patients. On the other hand, ventricular enlargement (which is characteristic of schizophrenia) has been observed in two of three studies. Much more work is clearly needed in this area.

Consistent with the notion of schizotypal personality disorder as a related and less severe manifestation of the liability towards schizophrenia, many (but not all) of the structural abnormalities present in schizophrenia are also apparent in schizotypal personality disorder. For example, individuals with schizotypal personality disorder show brain abnormalities in the superior temporal and parahippocampal gyri, lateral ventricles, thalamus, and septum pellucidum that are similar to those seen in persons with schizophrenia. However, medial temporal lobe abnormalities and lateral ventricular enlargement are not prominent in schizotypal personality disorder. If the structural differences observed between schizotypal personality disorder and schizophrenia relate directly to the clinical differences between the disorders, this would implicate enlargement of the ventricles and deterioration of the medial temporal lobes in the emergence of psychosis that separates the two disorders phenomenologically, but this hypothesis remains to be rigorously tested.

While structural brain imaging and postmortem tissue analysis have not yet been conducted on individuals with schizoid or paranoid personality disorders, the psychosis-risk state (which, after Paul Meehl, we reconceptualized as '**schizotaxia**') has received some attention, and findings of structural abnormalities in the non-psychotic relatives of individuals with schizophrenia are now becoming widely recognized. Compared with controls, this subgroup of relatives has significant volume reductions bilaterally in the amygdala-hippocampal region, thalamus, and cerebellum, and significantly increased volumes in the pallidum. Schizotaxic relatives of schizophrenic individuals may also exhibit lower volumes in other medial limbic and paralimbic structures, including the anterior cingulate and paracingulate cortex, insula, and parahippocampal gyrus.

Abnormalities of brain functioning

Whereas studies of brain *structure* look at the physical form and configuration of the brain, studies of brain *function* examine whether the brain is working correctly, regardless of its overall form and the configuration of its parts. A simple analogy helps to clarify the difference between brain structure and function. Consider an automobile engine that will not start. If a part, say the battery, is missing we conclude that the structure of the engine is abnormal. In contrast, if the battery is weak and the spark plugs are dirty we conclude that despite its normal structure, the engine has two specific defects in functioning.

The ability to study brain functioning in living people is perhaps one of the great contributions of neuroscience. To study the activity of the living brain, without harming the subject, was a monumental challenge. Fortunately, breakthroughs in medical technology have now made this possible. In fact, several methods of observing brain functioning were invented. Each of these suggests that individuals with schizophrenia have abnormalities of brain function.

In studies of regional cerebral blood flow (RCBF), scientists measure the amount of blood that is flowing to specific regions of the brain. Since the brain requires an ongoing supply of blood to work effectively, reduced blood flow indicates problems with brain functioning. Total brain blood flow is reduced in schizophrenia and regional blood flow measurements suggest a particular reduction in blood flow to the frontal cortex. The frontal cortex is the large portion of the brain at its front. It controls many aspects of human thought and emotion. In many ways it is the brain's supervisor because it coordinates and integrates the activities of other brain centers.

Positron emission tomography (PET) uses radioactive substances to measure the metabolism of the sugar glucose by specific parts of the brain. Since brain cells use glucose to function, reductions in glucose use indicate decreases in brain functioning. PET studies confirmed the findings of RCBF studies by showing a relative reduction in metabolic activity in the frontal cortex of individuals with schizophrenia compared with controls. These reductions were most notable when the patient performed a mental task during the procedure. This suggests that the schizophrenic brain cannot react to the world around it as quickly or as efficiently as a healthy brain.

A number of investigators think that the left side of the brain is particularly dysfunctional among individuals with schizophrenia. Originally this idea came from observations of one particular type of epilepsy (temporal epilepsy) in which abnormal brain waves arise from the temporal lobes at the sides of the brain. The word 'lobe' means 'region of the brain'. Sufferers from this form of epilepsy sometimes have symptoms indistinguishable from those of true schizophrenia. It seems that the temporal lobes may be involved in the production of certain schizophrenic features such as delusions, hallucinations, or disorganized thoughts. Furthermore, temporal lobe epilepsy involving primarily the left side of the brain tends to present more schizophrenic features, such as disorganized thoughts, whereas in temporal epilepsy involving the right side of the brain, symptoms of mood disorder are more common. This led to an intriguing idea: perhaps the left side of the brain was impaired in schizophrenia.

In support of this idea were reports that a relatively high proportion of individuals with schizophrenia are left-handed. This finding is relevant for the following reason. Most people are right-handed because the left side of their brain is dominant to the right side. Since the left brain controls the right hand (and the right brain controls the left hand), left-handedness may indicate that the left side of the brain is not functioning properly and therefore has lost its dominance over the right brain. This idea has received much attention because the left side of the brain is usually regarded as controlling language and thought and these are impaired in schizophrenia.

Overall, RCBF and PET studies lend some support to the idea that individuals with schizophrenia have a dysfunctional left brain and that they fail to shift mental processing to the right brain when appropriate. For example, one study found that the relative amount of blood flow to the left and right brains differentiated patients with schizophrenia from people without psychiatric problems. For a verbal task (controlled by the left brain), the patients showed no flow asymmetries. In contrast, the healthy subjects showed an increase in left brain flow. For a spatial task (controlled by the right brain) the patients showed greater left brain increases than right brain increases; the control subjects showed a larger right brain increase on the same task.

Another approach to brain imaging has been to look at the electrical activity of the brain. Since nerve cells in the brain communicate in a manner similar to electrical impulses, methods that measure the pattern of electrical activity can clarify brain functioning. The electroencephalogram (EEG) has a long history of use in schizophrenia studies. In the popular press, the EEG is often reported as the study of 'brain waves' because it records the electrical activity of the brain in a series of wavy lines. Twenty to forty per cent of individuals with schizophrenia have EEG recordings that are abnormal. These abnormalities are not related to the clinical features of the patients, their duration of illness, or the severity of their illness. The EEG abnormalities are usually observed on both the left and right sides of the brain. These deviant EEG patterns are not only seen in schizophrenia; we also see them in other psychiatric and neurological patients. However, the type of abnormality seen among individuals with schizophrenia differs from the epileptiform activity seen in patients with epilepsy.

A technologically more sophisticated descendant of the EEG is brain potential imaging (BPI). BPI is a newer electrophysiological technique that allows the electrical activity of several brain areas to be measured at one time. The result is an electrophysiological 'map' of brain functioning that allows for subtle comparisons between brain regions. BPI studies of individuals with schizophrenia are consistent with RCBF studies in finding evidence of relatively lower levels of brain activity in the frontal cortex compared with other brain regions.

The latest wave of functional neuroimaging studies to produce reliable facts about the schizophrenic brain involve functional MRI (fMRI) studies and diffusion tensor imaging (DTI) studies. DTI is a relatively new technology that measures the degree to which the brain's 'white matter' or nerve fibers (as opposed to 'grey matter' or cells) is intact. As recently as 2005, a comprehensive review of DTI studies of schizophrenia showed that a large majority of DTI studies of schizophrenia had found reduced 'anisotropy' in patients compared to unaffected control subjects. A reduction in anisotropy is taken to indicate that the nerve fibers in a particular tract are not properly aligned, and may reflect aberrations in axonal arborization or projection which could lead to inefficient transmission of nerve impulses between brain regions. Despite the high degree of uniformity found at the level of global anisotropy reductions in schizophrenia, to date there has been very little agreement between studies with regard to the particular tracts in the brain where deficits are most pronounced or most reliably detected.

fMRI couples the techniques of magnetic resonance imaging, which were described above in our review of structural brain abnormalities, and RCBF to spatially localize abnormal brain energy utilization patterns in discrete brain regions during the performance of a particular task, usually a neuropsychological task that draws largely on one or a few regions of the brain. This technique has even been used recently in the resting state to identify abnormalities in the so-called default network in schizophrenia, suggesting that functional neurobiological abnormalities in schizophrenia are present not only when the brain is taxed, but also when it is at rest. Consistent with other imaging modalities, the most routinely observed fMRI abnormalities in schizophrenia include a decrease in frontal lobe activity ('hypofrontality') during the performance of demanding cognitive tasks; however, more recently, some data have emerged to suggest that overall activity in the frontal lobes is not reduced but simply more dispersed in individuals with schizophrenia, suggesting less efficient processing and the notion that the schizophrenic brain must work harder to attain normal levels of performance. In the last decade, fMRI (which itself pairs two technologies) has been effectively paired with the methods of genetic association analysis by Dr Daniel Weinberger and others to identify the potential mechanisms by which schizophrenia susceptibility genes change the brain in people with schizophrenia. Among the most consistent observations in this line of investigation has been that of decreased neural efficiency (or recruitment of 'greater neuronal resources') in the prefrontal cortex of the brain in individuals with schizophrenia while they perform a working memory task.

This neurocognitive process has been shown by Dr Weinberger and others to be mediated by a schizophrenia-risk-associated polymorphism in the *COMT* gene, which encodes an enzyme (catechol-*o*-methyltransferase) that produces dopamine. This approach highlights a promising avenue by which genes that increase liability towards the disorder can be validated biologically to separate true effects from potential false-positive leads.

Collectively, functional studies of schizophrenia find abnormal patterns of brain activation that are generally confined to those regions in which structural abnormalities have also been noted, and the same may be true for the spectrum conditions as well, although, some anomalies in structure and function do not overlap in schizophrenia. It has been somewhat difficult to integrate all of the reports of functional brain abnormalities in schizophrenia due to methodological considerations. Most importantly, patterns of brain activation are influenced by the demands placed on the individuals during the imaging process. Thus, functional brain images acquired from people with schizophrenia performing a wide variety of tasks in different studies (e.g., a working memory task, an auditory vigilance task, and a verbal comprehension test) are not readily combinable. Furthermore, studies specifically seeking analogous deficits on consistently deficient processes in schizophrenia (e.g., motor task performance, verbal fluency, auditory attention) in patients with schizoaffective disorder or schizoid or paranoid personality disorders have yet to emerge; thus, although functional brain imaging is a powerful tool, it has yet to influence our understanding of most schizophrenia-spectrum disorders and their treatment, although there is little doubt that it will in the near future.

The exception to this generalization is schizotypal personality disorder, for which a small but important body of work exists. These reports of functional abnormalities in schizotypal personality disorder are so important because the picture that emerges seems to further justify the personality disorder's position along the schizophrenia spectrum. For example, some work indicates that abnormalities in frontal activation in schizotypal personality disorder mimic those of schizophrenia, but that alternative brain regions are recruited by schizotypal personality disordered individuals to help accomplish tasks requiring frontal lobe activation. Also, resting metabolic activity in dopamine-containing subcortical nuclei (particularly the putamen) is increased among schizotypal individuals relative to controls and individuals with schizophrenia, whereas during performance of a verbal working memory task (a domain that is among the most impaired in individuals with schizophrenia and among their non-psychotic relatives), individuals with schizotypal personality disorder exhibited reduced activation relative to controls.

As stated above, the functional integrity of the brain has not been investigated in individuals with schizoid personality disorder, and the evidence for functional abnormalities in paranoid personality disorder is essentially anecdotal at this point. For example, frontal lobe dysfunction has been reported to mimic paranoid personality in case studies. Schizotaxia, however, has received more attention in this regard, and findings of functional brain abnormalities in the non-psychotic relatives of individuals with schizophrenia appear to be robust and reliable. For example, the schizotaxic relatives of individuals with schizophrenia show abnormal brain activation patterns while performing working memory tasks with interference. Such tasks produce activation in the lateral and medial prefrontal cortex, posterior parietal and precuneal cortex, and thalamus in controls and schizotaxic individuals, but to a greater extent in the schizotaxic group. This increase in activation is not due to a greater intensity of activity, but to more widespread brain activation in the relatives. Furthermore, schizotaxic individuals may exhibit more bilateral activation on working memory tasks with or without interference than do control subjects. These findings indicate at least two possibilities: 1) schizotaxic individuals demonstrate a compensatory exertion of inefficient neural circuitry in attempting to perform an effortful task to produce accurate output, or 2) schizotaxic individuals have abnormal connectivity in the circuitry required to perform these tasks. These functional data complement the structural MRI abnormalities of schizotaxia, which jointly suggests that adult relatives of individuals with schizophrenia do indeed have brain abnormalities, possibly associated with abnormal genes.

Genetic heterogeneity and brain dysfunction in schizophrenia

The inconsistency of findings from different studies of the aetiology of schizophrenia has been taken as evidence for genetic heterogeneity in the causation of the disorder. This conclusion implies that several genetic forms of schizophrenia may exist, along with some non-genetic forms as well. A theoretical distinction has been made between people with schizophrenia having a family history of the disorder (familial cases) and those with no such family history (sporadic cases). Furthermore, some experimental evidence indicates that this division is valid and useful for identifying specific deficits that may be heritable. For example, measures of attention, particularly sustained attention or vigilance as measured by the continuous performance test (CPT), are impaired more often in familial cases of schizophrenia than in sporadic cases. Furthermore, it is quite interesting to note that poor attentional performance is consistently observed in the relatives of individuals with schizophrenia. However, differences in attention between familial and sporadic cases of schizophrenia are not always found, and people with familial schizophrenia actually outperform sporadic people with schizophrenia on a different measure of attention, the digit span task.

Evidence from electrophysiologic studies of the brains of people with schizophrenia suggests that these differences in attentional performance between familial and sporadic cases may have neurobiological bases. For example, familial cases are more likely to produce abnormal visual and auditory evoked potentials. In addition, some relatives of individuals with schizophrenia demonstrate evoked potential abnormalities. Thus, the relatives of individuals with schizophrenia show abnormalities in tests of sustained attention and in evoked potential recordings, deficits that were also found more commonly in familial cases of schizophrenia than in non-familial cases. In contrast, irregular EEGs are detected more frequently in sporadic cases than in familial cases.

The weight of evidence supports the notion that sporadic cases of schizophrenia exhibit more structural brain abnormalities than familial cases. This difference substantiated earlier work that found no difference in the ventricular size between concordant and discordant MZ twin pairs, but significantly larger ventricles in patients with no family history of the illness. Subsequently, the ventricular:brain ratio was found to be 21% greater in subjects with no family history of schizophrenia than in subjects with a positive family history of the disorder. Thus, the body of work indicates that there is an increase in ventricular volume in at least some non-familial individuals with schizophrenia.

The evidence for increased brain abnormalities in non-familial cases of schizophrenia suggests a major role for environmental factors in their aetiology. This hypothesis is further supported by findings from twin studies in which the affected members of discordant MZ twin pairs were found to have greater neurodiagnostic abnormalities than their unaffected co-twins. Specifically, the affected siblings generally had greater neuropsychological dysfunction, larger cerebral ventricles, more abnormalities in brain MRIs, and greater 'hypofrontality'. Because MZ twins are genetically identical, such differences between the members of these twin-pairs must be due to environmental factors.

Dr Tyrone Cannon first proposed that obstetric complications (OCs) might combine with the genetic predisposition to schizophrenia to produce these structural brain abnormalities. Within a high-risk sample, there were linear increases in the ratios of cortex and ventricular cerebrospinal fluid to whole brain as the level of genetic liability to schizophrenia increased. Furthermore, the effect of OCs on ventricular size increased as the level of genetic risk for schizophrenia increased, such that OCs had little effect on this measure in subjects with two normal parents, a larger effect in those with one schizophrenic parent, and the largest impact on those individuals with two affected parents.

A full understanding of the aetiology and pathophysiology of schizophrenia is presently obscured by the heterogeneity of the disorder. However, this obstacle may be overcome if more intensive research efforts are directed at this issue. Currently, attempts are being made to isolate homogenous subgroups of individuals with schizophrenia based on clinical features and neurobiological measures. Ultimately this work may facilitate our understanding of the course and outcome of schizophrenia, as well as the role of psychosocial factors in these processes. Changes in diagnostic nomenclature resulting from this work should also improve the ability of clinicians to choose the most effective treatment regimens for different subgroups of individuals with schizophrenia. Until these goals have been realized, the most effective treatment of schizophrenic disorders must continue to be derived from an extensive knowledge of the individual patient, clinical skill, and compassion.

Neuropsychological measures of brain functioning

The physiological measures of brain functioning discussed above provide clear evidence that the schizophrenic brain does not function correctly. However, because they measure physical aspects of the brain, they tell us little about how brain abnormalities in schizophrenia affect the patient's behaviour. The study of how brain abnormalities affect behaviour is a subspecialty of psychology known as 'neuropsychology'. In a neuropsychological study of schizophrenia, the neuropsychologist asks the patient to perform many tasks. These tasks are designed to measure specific aspects of brain functioning. For example, to test verbal memory the neuropsychologist may read a story and then ask the patient questions to see if key points are remembered. To test visual memory we show the patient designs and see if they can be recalled.

Most of us are familiar with the concept of intelligence. To a neuropsychologist, intelligence summarizes a person's overall level of brain functioning. In lay terms, it tells us how smart a person is when asked to do mental tasks. Patients with schizophrenia perform more poorly than healthy subjects on standardized intelligence tests. *On average*, the intelligence quotients (IQs) of individuals with schizophrenia are five to ten points lower than normal. We emphasize 'on average' because many patients with schizophrenia have normal IQs and some healthy people have IQs lower than some patients. Nevertheless, the lower average IQ scores of people with schizophrenia suggest that the abnormalities of brain structure and function discussed above lead to decreased abilities to perform mental tasks. The goal of neuropsychological studies has been to separate the abilities that are impaired in individuals with schizophrenia from those that are not.

Attention is a common word with many meanings to the lay person. The neuropsychologist breaks down the everyday idea of attention into several categories. **Immediate attention** is the ability to focus on a task for a short period of time. **Sustained attention** assesses the ability to focus on a task for a long period of time. We also speak of **selective attention,** the ability to focus on one thing (e.g., a conversation) while ignoring another (e.g., background music). People with schizophrenia show problems in each of these areas of attention. In general, their ability to attend becomes worse as the task becomes more difficult.

Motor abilities refer to the coordination of thinking and muscles to accomplish a task. One aspect of motor functioning is speed. How quickly can a task be done? In most studies, patients with schizophrenia are consistently slower than normal. It is difficult for the neuropsychologist to know if this slowness is due to problems with attention or other abilities. Whatever the cause of this slow response speed, it makes it difficult for patients with schizophrenia to work as efficiently as a healthy person. Thus, it is one of the many reasons they find it difficult to maintain steady employment.

Deficits in **abstraction** and **concept formation** have long been observed among individuals with schizophrenia. Both of these are necessary components of effective, higher level thinking. *Abstraction* is the ability to move from the specific, observable aspects of life to general principles. The most straightforward example is concept formation whereby we group items together. This may be as simple as knowing that mice, cats, and dogs are all animals; but concept formation can be very complex, as in learning the boundaries of ethical behaviour. More importantly, these functions are closely related to the planning and organizational skills we need in everyday life. It is not surprising that many people with schizophrenia do poorly on these tasks since clinical observations show them to be deficient in many of these skills. Notably, their poor performance on these tasks is related to reduced activity of the frontal cortex measured in brain blood flow studies. Thus, the neuropsychological studies are consistent with the imaging studies discussed above.

Our clinical descriptions of schizophrenia noted that thought disorder is a common schizophrenic symptom. Thus, it is not surprising that these patients also have difficulties with neuropsychological measures of **verbal ability** and **language.** Yet these problems are different from the speech and language problems that neurologists describe in many neurology patients. For example, individuals with schizophrenia usually have mild language disturbances in which simple language functions like naming objects and understanding speech are not affected. These simple functions are often disturbed in people with neurological conditions. In contrast, individuals with schizophrenia usually have problems with complex language tasks.

As we all know from everyday experience, **learning and memory** are essential mental activities, which we use on a regular basis. Research consistently finds that patients with schizophrenia have difficulties with learning and memory.

They have learning and memory problems for both verbal information (words, sentences, and stories) and for visual information (pictures). In both these areas, the memory deficits are seen if patients are asked to remember items over short or long periods of time.

Patients with schizophrenia tend to do reasonably well on simple **visual-spatial** tasks. These tasks require the patient to observe a problem and determine its solution based on the spatial relationships of items that are seen. For example, organizing a group of blocks to match a design is a visual-spatial task. Relative to other neuropsychological skills, visual-spatial functioning appears to be less impaired in schizophrenia. This finding may be related to the issue of **brain asymmetry**. This is a complicated issue since it involves knowledge of how the normal human brain is organized. A simplified, yet essentially correct, description is as follows. The brain is composed of two halves, left and right, which look very similar to one another. If you cut an orange in half, the two halves would look like one another. Thus, we say the orange is symmetrical. The human brain, with some exceptions, is physically symmetrical. However, it is functionally asymmetrical. By this we mean that the left and right brains control different mental tasks. Most notably, the left brain is responsible for processing language. It thinks in a logical, sequential manner. In contrast, the right brain processes non-linguistic material. We use it for visual-spatial and other tasks that require us to think 'without language'. For example, if we ask you to copy a design you are likely to make the copy without talking to yourself about the specific features of the design you are copying. When a mental function is performed by one half of the brain we say that the function is 'lateralized' or exhibits 'brain laterality'.

Abnormalities in brain laterality are found in some individuals with schizophrenia. Studies usually find these patients have greater left brain than right brain dysfunction. As we discussed above, they tend to have problems with verbal and language abilities (a function of the left brain), but not with visual-spatial abilities (a function of the right brain). Individuals with schizophrenia are also more likely to be left-handed, which may be a sign of abnormal brain laterality. However, most are right-handed. Thus, the unusual patterns of brain asymmetry seen in schizophrenia probably indicate relatively small differences in left and right brain functioning. That is, in schizophrenia the left side of the brain is not completely useless, but it does not function as efficiently as the right side.

Neurotransmitter dysfunction

The studies we have discussed so far show that the brains of individuals with schizophrenia do not function correctly. They do not, however, tell us the causes of this dysfunction. For example, we do not believe that decreased blood flow, abnormal glucose use, or neuropsychological phenomena cause schizophrenia. Instead, they are best thought of as indices of brain function that are affected by the disease process that causes schizophrenia. Ideally, we would know what causes these brain abnormalities since that might lead us to the ultimate cause of schizophrenia.

Many scientists have proposed that the underlying cause of schizophrenia can be found within the neurotransmitter systems of the brain. To make this clear, we must provide a brief overview of how these systems work. The brain is composed of thousands of brain cells called neurons. These neurons collect information from the five senses and relay it to other neurons in the brain for mental processing. These neurons, in turn, may relay the information to one or more areas of the brain for additional mental processing. To relay information, a neuron must send a chemical message to another neuron.

Neurons are separated by a small gap called the 'synapse'. To send a message to the second neuron, the first one must release a chemical called a neuro-transmitter. This neurotransmitter travels across the synapse and eventually lands on little platforms, called receptors, which are attached to the second neuron. When enough of these platforms are occupied, an electrical signal is created in the second neuron that corresponds to the message being sent. When the size of this electrical signal exceeds a threshold, an electrical impulse is sent across the second neuron. In this manner, the neurons in the brain talk to one another and control all the functions of our mind and body.

The chemical communication of the synapse is a remarkable system which usually works very efficiently. However, there are several ways in which a disease can interfere with this process. For example, the first neuron may not produce enough chemical, it may produce too much chemical, or it may produce the wrong chemical. A problem could also occur with the second neuron. It may not have enough receptors or it may have too many. Also, if the shape of the receptor is wrong then the chemical released by the first neuron might not be able to land. Thus, a common theme of the neurotransmitter theories of schiz-ophrenia is that imbalances in the concentration of neurotransmitters or abnormal activities at the synapse cause the illness.

Although many functional imaging methods measure 'brain activation' by quantifying energy consumption, the functional abnormalities in the brains of individuals with schizophrenia do not simply reflect a different pattern of blood flow or oxygenation, or glucose utilization (although these may be indicated). Rather, these differences are thought to be the observable conse-quence of altered neurotransmission. Thus, by proxy, functional brain imaging differences give some indication of underlying neurochemical and neurophys-iological pathology.

For decades, the central dopamine systems were considered the prime neural substrates of schizophrenic symptoms, and with good reason; the evidence supporting dopaminergic dysfunction in schizophrenia is voluminous. The 'dopamine hypothesis' of schizophrenia pathology was derived partly from observations that typical antipsychotic medications blocked dopamine D2 receptors, while indirect dopamine agonists like amphetamine produced psychotic symptoms that resembled schizophrenia. The initial and most basic form of the dopamine hypothesis asserted that schizophrenia results from dopaminergic hyperactivity, i.e., too much dopamine. Later reformulations focused on relationships between hyperactivity in mesolimbic dopamine neurons and dopaminergic hypoactivity in the prefrontal cortex. Although an exclusively dopaminergic hypothesis of schizophrenia is likely to be too simplistic to explain the development of the disorder, there is considerable (although, necessarily, indirect) evidence for both cortical dopaminergic hypoactivity and subcortical dopaminergic hyperactivity in schizophrenia.

Neuroimaging techniques offer perhaps the best current methods for examining aspects of neurotransmission non-invasively. Methods such as positron emission tomography and single-photon emission computerized tomography are not capable of visualizing actual neurotransmission, but can provide indirect indices of such by selectively measuring the occupancy of particular proteins in specific neurotransmitter pathways. The application of such methods has, to date, illustrated that dopamine transporter occupancy is not altered in schizophrenia, even early in the disease process, or in patients experiencing their first psychotic episode. Dopamine D2 receptors, however, have been reliably found to be occupied to a greater extent in individuals with schizophrenia than in controls, and at least a subset of patients exhibits greater D2 receptor density. Serotonin 2A receptors and gamma-amino butyric acid A receptors do not appear to be reliably altered in the schizophrenic brain.

The diversity of clinical symptoms in schizophrenia, the overwhelming evidence for a multifactorial polygenic aetiology, the multiple neurochemical actions of atypical antipsychotic medications such as clozapine, and the demonstration of numerous neurochemical and morphological abnormalities all underlie the view that multiple biochemical deficits contribute to the aetiology of schizophrenia. Thus, aside from dopaminergic dysfunction, abnormalities in glutamate neurotransmission are becoming central to working hypotheses of the pathology of schizophrenia. Much of this attention is derived from the fact that glutamate is a ubiquitous excitatory neurotransmitter in the central nervous system, which allows it to interact with many other transmitter systems, including dopamine (thus, dopamine dysfunction is presumed to follow from glutamatergic dysfunction). N-methyl-D-aspartate and α-amino-3-hydroxy-5-methyl-4-isoxasolepropionate glutamate receptors in the nucleus accumbens modulate dopaminergic neurons in the nucleus accumbens and in the frontal cortex, but the effect of glutamate differs at the two sites. The presence of presynaptic glutamate receptors on dopamine neurons in the frontal cortex generally results in facilitation of dopamine function, while dopamine reuptake is inhibited and release facilitated by glutamate in the nucleus accumbens. This means that agents that interfere with glutamate transmission would facilitate cortical dopaminergic hypoactivity and subcortical hyperactivity, which is consistent with the dopamine hypothesis of schizophrenia.

Further evidence for a role of glutamate in schizophrenia is derived from the fact that it is a critical neural substrate of cortical-level processing and cognition, and manipulations of glutamatergic function in schizophrenia reduce negative symptoms and improve cognition. In fact, glutamatergic antagonists, such as phencyclidine, elicit psychotic symptoms from non-schizophrenic individuals that resemble the illness, and they exacerbate symptoms in patients with schizophrenia. Phencyclidine acts by binding to a site on the N-methyl-D-aspartate receptor that blocks the influx of calcium and other cations through the ion channel, which then blocks receptor function. The effects of N-methyl-D-aspartate antagonists are not limited to positive symptoms. Phencyclidine and ketamine (another glutamatergic antagonist), for example, produce negative symptoms and cognitive deficits in verbal declarative memory and executive functions in normal subjects. Furthermore, administration of ketamine to patients with schizophrenia worsens psychotic symptoms and neuropsychological deficits.

Although there are many reports of dopaminergic and glutamatergic dysfunction in schizophrenia, scientists still debate the nature of these disruptions. One of the major questions regarding the role of these neurotransmitters in schizophrenia is cause or consequence. Because of the non-invasive techniques that must be used to study individuals with schizophrenia, and the fact that schizophrenic subjects are necessarily unavailable until they become ill, it has been difficult to establish whether the dopaminergic abnormalities reported by scientists precede the illness and contribute to its genesis, or are a consequence of the effects of disease onset, psychosis, or its pharmacological treatments. Generally, studies of non-medicated, first-episode patients have confirmed that these abnormalities are largely in place before illness onset, but additional longitudinal work currently under way in first-episode patients will need to be evaluated before this conclusion is considered definitive.

Studies of the non-psychotic schizotaxic relatives of patients with schizophrenia are useful for evaluating the timeline of neurotransmitter dysfunction in schizophrenia, since these individuals, by definition, have not suffered any psychotic symptoms or taken any psychopharmacologic medications. Thus, differences between schizotaxic individuals and normal controls can be viewed as a consequence of the underlying predisposition towards illness rather than as a function of the emergence of the disorder or its treatment. For example, the first-degree relatives of individuals with schizophrenia show lower circulating levels of the dopamine metabolite homovanillic acid when compared to a normal control group. Remarkably, plasma homovanillic acid is also inversely correlated with negative symptom scores and positively correlated with attenuated positive symptom scores on the Positive and Negative Syndrome Scale. The inverse correlation with negative symptom scores (i.e., higher levels of negative symptoms associated with lower levels of homovanillic acid) is particularly consistent with the diagnostic criterion of elevated negative symptoms in schizotaxia. However, it is important to note that it has not yet been determined if individuals who meet diagnostic criteria for schizotaxia show more, less, or the same amount of homovanillic acid reductions as fully normal relatives of individuals with schizophrenia. Furthermore, glutamatergic dysfunction in schizotaxia has yet to be investigated in depth.

Research on the biochemical basis of schizophrenia is often performed on subjects with either schizophrenia or schizoaffective disorder; thus, results from the two diagnostic categories have not traditionally been reported separately and, unfortunately, the neurochemical basis of schizoaffective disorder has yet to be investigated separately from schizophrenia. As a consequence, our knowledge of what differentiates schizoaffective disorder from schizophrenia at the biochemical level is lacking.

The quantity and quality of studies on neurotransmission in schizotypal personality disorder is also less than remarkable. In one study, plasma levels of homovanillic acid were increased among patients with schizotypal personality disorder relative to controls, but, as mentioned above, this is a very indirect measure of central dopaminergic activity. Cerebrospinal fluid levels of homovanillic acid were also reportedly elevated in patients with schizotypal personality disorder relative to those with other personality disorders, and psychotic-like schizotypal symptoms were correlated with homovanillic acid concentrations. These data are interesting, but they do not allow easy discrimination between two possible interpretations: 1) schizotypal personality disordered subjects exhibit the same trends as schizophrenic subjects relative to controls; or 2) homovanillic acid levels in schizotypal personality disorder are no different than those of controls, while the levels in subjects with other personality disorders are merely decreased relative to both groups. Neurochemical data on patients with schizoid or paranoid personality disorders are notably lacking altogether.

Schizophrenia research is evolving towards molecular methods, which promise to shed light upon the pathology of the disease and, ultimately, its aetiology. However, the true molecular aetiology of schizophrenia is only slowly being uncovered, and, as is typical, research into the molecular biological bases of schizophrenia-spectrum disorders will likely lag behind. Examination of these disorders at increasingly microscopic levels of analysis, including genomic and proteomic levels, will be necessary before their true foundations will be revealed. The challenge for the coming years will be to further clarify the specific pathological proteins that give rise to these disorders as a means to illuminate their common etiologic components. Such data will provide the basis for understanding how environmental and biological factors combine to influence one's placement along the schizophrenia spectrum, and, in addition, will facilitate the effective—but targeted—treatment of each condition as a separate entity that dictates a specific management strategy.

9

Is schizophrenia a neurodevelopmental disorder?

> ## ➡ Key points
>
> ◆ Neurodegenerative disorders occur when the causes of a disease attack and degrade a normal brain.
>
> ◆ Neurodevelopmental disorders occur when the causes of a disease stop the brain from developing normally.
>
> ◆ Schizophrenia appears to be a neurodevelopmental disorder, not a neurodegenerative one.
>
> ◆ The relatively late onset of schizophrenia (typically in the late teens and early 20s) may be preceded by years of subtle signs and abnormalities that do not garner clinical attention but are nonetheless indicative of abnormal neurodevelopment.
>
> ◆ Stress or other environmental factors in early adulthood may precipitate illness in a neurodevelopmentally compromised individual.

The research we have discussed suggests that schizophrenia occurs when abnormal genes and environmental risk factors combine to cause brain dysfunction. In the past decade, several researchers—notably Drs Daniel Weinberger, Larry Seidman, and Patricia Goldman Rakic—have concluded that schizophrenia is a neurodevelopmental brain disorder.

To understand this concept, it is useful to consider brain disorders that do not have a neurodevelopmental origin. We call these disorders neurodegenerative because the causes of the disease attack and degrade a normal brain. The senility of old age, which doctors call dementia, is a common example. When some people age, their brain is degraded by events such as many strokes or the ravages of Alzheimer's disease. After a few years, a person who once functioned normally can no longer do simple tasks. Other examples are acquired brain syndromes, which occur after an injury to the head, and disorders due to the ingestion of toxic substances (e.g., drugs, lead paint). In each of these cases, some external agent has acted on a normal brain to make it abnormal.

In contrast, in neurodevelopmental disorders, the brain does not develop (i.e., grow) properly. In other words, it was never really normal to begin with. We know that genes contain the 'blueprint' for building the brain. For schizophrenia, this blueprint contains errors so that the brain is not 'built' correctly. Dr Patricia Goldman Rakic suggested that certain brain cells in individuals with schizophrenia do not 'migrate' correctly during development. That is, normal brain development requires that cells locate themselves in the right spot and connect to one another in specific patterns. In schizophrenia, it may be that some cells are in the wrong place, some do not make necessary connections and others make connections that should not be made. It is as if the blueprint for a home told the electrician to put the light switch for the kitchen in the living room.

As we discussed before, schizophrenia genes and early environmental risk factors such as pregnancy complications may lead to abnormal brain development. If so, then why does the disorder lie dormant for many years? The average age at onset for schizophrenia is between 18 and 25 for men and 26–45 for women. If the brain's blueprint is wrong, shouldn't we see more schizophrenia in childhood?

Schizophrenia researchers are currently seeking detailed answers to these questions. In the meanwhile, we can provide partial answers. First, recall the studies discussed in previous chapters describing children of schizophrenic mothers as having deviant scores on neuropsychological measures of brain functioning. Drs Barbara Fish and Joseph Marcus showed that among such children, those who eventually developed schizophrenia had measurable neurologic abnormalities. These studies showed that the brains of individuals with schizophrenia were not normal in childhood, well before the onset of the illness.

The brain abnormalities of pre-schizophrenic children probably impair their functioning at school and make it difficult to form friendships. Dr Elaine Walker collected the home movies made of individuals with schizophrenia when they were children, prior to their first schizophrenic episode. The movies also recorded some children who did not develop schizophrenia. Dr Walker had psychology graduate students and experienced clinicians view these movies with the goal of deciding which children in the movies eventually became schizophrenic. Although they made some errors, these raters were able to classify many of the children correctly. This study suggests that, although these children would not develop schizophrenia for many years, their social behaviour was unusual enough to be detected by the study's raters.

These studies indicate that the pre-schizophrenic child shows abnormal behaviours, which suggests that the pre-schizophrenic brain is also abnormal. But why does the onset of schizophrenia usually occur in late adolescence or adulthood? One answer is that the brain's development takes some time. Although much of it is complete at birth, the brain continues to develop throughout childhood and adolescence. Moreover, the last part to complete development is the frontal cortex. This area of the brain is involved in some of our most complex types of thinking and behaviour and is one that brain imaging studies show to be abnormal in schizophrenia.

Thus, the onset of schizophrenia may need to wait for certain areas of the brain to develop incorrectly. When these brain areas cannot perform functions necessary for people to cope with the transition from adolescence to adulthood or with the challenges of adulthood, schizophrenia may ensue. However, many patients onset in their late 20s and early 30s, long after the brain has completed its development. These later onsets suggest that environmental factors may need to stress the abnormal pre-schizophrenic brain before symptoms of the disorder appear.

10

How is schizophrenia treated?

➜ Key points

◆ Although not a 'cure' for the disorder, for many patients, neuroleptic medications effectively control the positive symptoms of schizophrenia.

◆ Neuroleptics can cause severe side effects, including involuntary motor movements and restlessness.

◆ Second-generation, or atypical, antipsychotic medications such as clozapine are also effective for reducing schizophrenia symptoms, with a lower side effect burden than first-generation neuroleptics; however, other side effects may be encountered, such as metabolic syndrome and, rarely, more serious side effects such as agranulocytosis which can be deadly; thus, careful monitoring is required.

◆ The largest and most comprehensive comparative studies have found clozapine to be slightly more effective than other second-generation antipsychotics, whereas ziprasidone has the fewest side effects.

At this point the reader may be frustrated with the uncertainty that tinges our discussion of schizophrenia. In earlier chapters we have chronicled the many advances in our understanding of schizophrenia. Unfortunately, we still do not have a detailed blueprint of what exactly goes wrong in the schizophrenic brain and why the brain cannot recover. Nevertheless, we must help patients and their families to relieve their suffering. It is no use saying, 'We cannot help you, since we still do not know the exact nature of schizophrenia' or 'More research needs to be done first,' as patients and their relatives desperately need some sort of help now.

Of course, more research is needed to evaluate methods of treatment for schizophrenia and to find its ultimate causes. But, for the time being, we must apply currently available knowledge as best we can. However, we must not burden patients and their families with ineffective or counterproductive methods of treatment. As therapists, whenever we are in a dilemma about what to suggest for a patient because of conflicting evidence, or lack of it, from research data, we should always ask ourselves, 'If this patient were a close relative of ours, what would we do?' We think the insight this self-questioning provides is very useful for clinicians in all fields of medicine.

What brings patients to treatment?

The onset of schizophrenia frightens patients and their families. Patients begin to express many odd beliefs: that people are trying to harm them—friends, relatives, strangers, or celebrities; that others can hear their thoughts as if spoken aloud; that voices talk to them, even when they are alone. In addition, they cannot express feelings and thoughts clearly and are frustrated by the disbelief of relatives and friends. They can sense that something is wrong, but do not see themselves as a patient who needs professional help. Well-meaning relatives and friends try to reason with them, but such discussions often deteriorate into arguments or heated disputes.

Relatives struggle with the patient's bizarre schizophrenic beliefs, unreasonable behaviours, and increasing isolation. When they ask the individual to seek medical help they are often disappointed. To the patient, bizarre beliefs reflect reality, not the effects of a brain disease. Some affected individuals seek treatment on their own, but usually for a bizarre reason. For example, one of our patients came to the emergency room asking doctors to remove a radio transmitter from his brain. Another complained to a dentist that the Central Intelligence Agency had put computer chips in her teeth. Another sought relief from the rats that were eating his intestines. In some cases, relatives convince the patient that a trip to the family doctor might prove useful.

Even when patients eventually see a doctor, they may become very upset when the doctor suggests a psychiatric consultation. Indeed, relatives, friends, and even the doctor may become persecutors in their delusional systems. At this stage, we try to prevent further deterioration by persuading patients to be admitted to hospital for an examination. In most cases, they can be persuaded to accept hospitalization. If they refuse, and are dangerous to themselves or others, then involuntary admission through legal commitment procedures may be necessary. The legal commitment process can be slow and frustrating to family members who see the dire need for the patient to be hospitalized. Judges understand the urgency of these issues, but their duty to the law requires that they be extremely careful not to take away a patient's right to liberty without clear documentation that the patient is indeed dangerous to themselves or to others.

Treatment begins with diagnosis

When patients are extremely upset or when their behaviour is out of control, the doctor may suggest an emergency treatment. By calming the patient, this takes care of the immediate problem and helps the doctor collect the information needed to make a diagnosis. When the diagnosis is complete, the doctor will prepare a treatment plan.

Many patients—and even their relatives—become annoyed at the time it takes to make a diagnosis. The doctor will request many medical tests: X-rays, blood tests, and other physical examinations. These are needed to be sure that the apparent symptoms of schizophrenia are not due to some other physical illness. It would be a tragic mistake if the doctor did not learn that street drugs, a brain tumour, or some other problem had caused the schizophrenic symptoms because the method of treating these conditions would be different than the treatment of schizophrenia having no known cause. With the results of laboratory tests they will rule out any disorders due to causes that can mimic schizophrenia. We use this process of elimination because there is no positive laboratory test for schizophrenia yet.

The diagnostic process takes additional time to carefully examine patients, and their histories, to detect any of the symptoms that are usually associated with typical schizophrenia. At most hospitals, a team of professionals work together to make the diagnosis: social workers enquire about the patient's family life, psychologists administer tests of personality and intellectual ability, doctors and nurses take a detailed medical and family history. Some, or all, of these professionals will talk to friends and family to collect additional information. To many, the team of professionals trying to help the patients is daunting. Their interviews and tests may seem tedious and repetitious. Their roles on the treatment team may be unclear. We suggest that patients and relatives clear up such misunderstandings. Most professionals will be pleased to explain what they do and how it relates to the work of other team members.

We have found that patients and their relatives often confuse psychologists with psychiatrists. They wonder: why do I need two doctors? Psychiatrists are physicians that have received specialty training in the diagnosis and medical treatment of mental illness. Their training allows them to prescribe drugs and to monitor their effects on the patient's mental and physical systems. Psychologists are not physicians, and, with rare exceptions, cannot prescribe drugs. They are trained to assess psychopathology and its effects on thinking and emotion. They are specially trained to treat schizophrenia using largely psychological and behavioural techniques.

Throughout the diagnostic process, patients and family members must remember a key point: the treatment of an individual with apparent schizophrenia is unlikely to be successful until a comprehensive diagnostic work-up is completed. Only then can the patient's treatment team prepare an optimal treatment plan.

Medical treatment

Since schizophrenia is a brain disease, the reader will not be surprised to learn that its primary medical treatment requires drugs that influence brain functioning. Before we tell you what these drugs are, let us be certain that you know what they are not.

Psychiatric drugs are not cures for schizophrenia. Most patients improve, some do not. Few go on to live normal lives: milder symptoms may always remain and episodes of severe schizophrenia may return. Nevertheless, the quality of life for patients and their families is usually much better with drug treatment than without.

Psychiatric drugs are not 'chemical strait jackets'. We frequently hear lay people refer to psychiatric drugs with such pejorative terms. This view portrays medicine as mind control. In the extreme, it accuses psychiatrists of stripping the creativity and individuality away from the person with schizophrenia, of making them helpless to control their own destinies. This is nonsense. Nothing could be further from the truth. Psychiatric medicine corrects brain functioning to help patients think clearly and better control their lives. Without medical help, the patient's personality disintegrates into a morass of fear and fantasy. With medical help, recovery begins.

Neuroleptic drugs

Neuroleptic or **antipsychotic** drugs are a group of medicines that have similar chemical properties. Because of their chemical make-up, they can alleviate some symptoms of schizophrenia. Doctors usually prescribe them when the patient has active schizophrenic symptoms such as delusions or hallucinations. At this stage, the patients are so totally out of touch with reality that they cannot correctly perceive efforts to help them. Neuroleptic drugs break down the barriers of emotion and communication disturbance that separate patients from their friends, relatives, and therapists. Since the 1950s, when these drugs were first introduced, worldwide studies have shown their effectiveness in treating schizophrenic symptoms. On average, two-thirds of patients show a significant improvement, and approximately 25% show no or little improvement.

The doctor's first choice of a neuroleptic drug for a patient will be guided by all the information, both medical and psychological, collected during the diagnostic work-up. In almost all cases, the use of a single type is preferred to a 'cocktail' of several. Of course, additional medicines may be prescribed to deal with other medical problems, and sometimes more than one medication might be required to treat the patient's schizophrenia. Unfortunately, there is no way for the doctor to be certain that his first choice will be correct. The drug may be ineffective, or the patient may suffer from severe side effects.

In such cases we urge the patient to try another drug. The workings of the brain are complex and our knowledge about schizophrenia is incomplete. Although the group of neuroleptic medications are similar to one another, where one fails another may succeed. This is the clinical experience of many psychiatrists. Thus, patients and their families should be neither discouraged nor alarmed if their doctor tries a sequence of medications before relief is achieved and side effects are controlled. This is common in the treatment of schizophrenia since we have no way of knowing which specific neuroleptic will be effective for any given patient.

Neuroleptic side effects

Unfortunately, neuroleptic drugs bring with them the risk of side effects. These range from the unpleasant to the debilitating. In very rare circumstances, death can occur. Many of these problems can be avoided or controlled if the patient remains in the care of a psychiatrist.

We call the most common side effects of neuroleptics '**extrapyramidal**' symptoms because they are due to the action of these drugs on the brain's extrapyramidal system. This neural system helps control movement. The three basic types of extrapyramidal symptoms—**dystonia, akathisia,** and **pseudoparkinsonism**—occur in 40–60% of patients. Dystonic reactions are involuntary muscle contractions, typically involving muscles of the head and face. These muscle contractions are uncomfortable, and sometimes painful. They make the patient feel stiff. Because facial appearance and body posture may be distorted, the patient is embarrassed in social situations.

Akathisia is a subjective feeling of restlessness. It may be physically expressed by pacing, rocking from foot to foot, other motor activity, or insomnia. Ranging from mild to extremely irritating, it, like other side effects, may lead patients to stop taking their medicine. Pseudoparkinsonism is a condition that is virtually indistinguishable from the neurological disease called Parkinson's disease. It includes tremors, stiffness, and, sometimes, lack of movement. The patient's face may show little expressiveness, as if he were wearing a mask.

The extrapyramidal side effects usually occur within a few days of treatment with neuroleptics. Fortunately, the psychiatrist often can relieve these problems. One approach is to switch to another neuroleptic drug. Another possibility is to treat the patient with drugs that are specifically designed to control the side effects. Patients and their families should discuss these symptoms with the psychiatrist. Two key points must be remembered. First, these side effects are not a worsening of schizophrenic symptoms. They are well-known effects of neuroleptic drugs. Second, such problems should not lead to questioning the competence of the psychiatrist. Unfortunately, medical knowledge can predict neither which patients will develop side effects nor how severe these will be.

If neuroleptics are used over a long period, a neurological complication, called **tardive dyskinesia**, may develop. Like extrapyramidal conditions, tardive dyskinesia produces uncontrollable muscle movements, usually of the face. Patients with tardive dyskinesia repeatedly smack their lips together, stick out their tongue, grimace, and move their chin from side to side. These are not as easily reversed as extrapyramidal symptoms, particularly in older patients. Withdrawal of neuroleptics may stop the dyskinetic movements. However, in some cases the syndrome will not stop, even when neuroleptic drugs are taken away.

Research studies suggest that approximately 20% of neuroleptic-treated patients will develop tardive dyskinesia. However, we have no way of knowing, prior to treatment, which these patients are. Thus, neuroleptic treatment must be overseen by a psychiatrist or other physician experienced and skilled in their use. Careful, periodic observations of the patient help the psychiatrist spot tardive dyskinesia in its earliest stages when it is easiest to treat.

Neuroleptic malignant syndrome is a severe side effect of neuroleptic treatment. Fortunately, it is very rare. The clinical signs of the syndrome are fever, a fast heartbeat, muscle stiffness, altered consciousness, abnormal blood pressure, shortness of breath, and sweating. If the psychiatrist suspects neuroleptic malignant syndrome, a blood test will be used to see if he is correct. If the patient has abnormal levels of specific constituents of blood, then neuroleptic malignant syndrome is likely. Because this syndrome will lead to death, the neuroleptic drug will be taken away from the patient. This will reverse the syndrome.

Low-dose neuroleptic treatment

After realizing that neuroleptic side effects were frequent—and that some were severe—clinical scientists sought to develop new dosing strategies. Their goal was to give patients the smallest amount of neuroleptic that would have a therapeutic effect. The cornerstone of this new treatment philosophy was that, during their lifetime, patients should take only that amount of medicine that was medically necessary.

These scientists quickly learned that excessive usage of neuroleptics occurs when the dose needed to help a very ill patient is not reduced after the most severe and distressing symptoms have subsided. When individuals with schizophrenia are very psychotic and agitated, the doctor will usually prescribe a relatively high dose of neuroleptic. However, clinical scientists have shown that these high doses are not always needed after the initial psychosis and agitation subsides. Since these drugs have serious side effects, we cannot justify the extended use of large doses without evidence that lower doses are not effective.

The patient and family must understand that before treatment, the doctor cannot know what dose is ideal. Due to differences in physiology, different people may require very different doses to achieve the same clinical effect. Thus, the doctor who changes doses several times is not being erratic, but merely trying to find the optimal dose.

Ideally, drug treatment should be reduced soon after the initial symptoms are relieved. This long-term treatment, which continues after discharge from the hospital, is often called 'maintenance' treatment because it helps maintain the patient in the community. We emphasize that, although maintenance treatment is very effective, it cannot guarantee that severe symptoms will not return. After 2 years, approximately half the individuals with schizophrenia who have been on drug maintenance treatment will relapse. This is a sobering statistic, yet it compares favourably with an 84% relapse rate in patients who have not been treated.

During outpatient treatment, two strategies are available: low-dose treatment and intermittent treatment. With a low-dose strategy patients are maintained on a dose that is much lower than that initially required. In some cases this is as much as 90% less. More intensive treatment is reserved for periods of symptom worsening. The maintenance dose of medication that will keep target symptoms reduced to a satisfactory level is highly individual and can be determined only by trial and error. The intermittent medication strategy withdraws all medication during periods of remission and uses neuroleptics only when the patient appears to be at risk for relapse. This requires frequent observation of the patient by the family and by clinicians so that early signs of a pending relapse will signal a protective increase in medication.

'Atypical' or 'second-generation' antipsychotics

After neuroleptics were in use for a while, the next big breakthrough in the drug treatment of schizophrenia was the discovery of the so-called atypical or second-generation antipsychotics, such as risperidone, olanzapine, quetiapine, sertindole, and ziprasidone. These drugs differ from traditional neuroleptics in several ways. Some of these are advantageous. For example, they have relatively few extrapyramidal side effects and can therefore provide relief for patients who cannot tolerate the side effects of other drugs. Patients using these drugs are also less likely to develop tardive dyskinesia. More importantly, these are effective in many patients who are not helped by other neuroleptics. This is especially true for clozapine, which has the strongest evidence of helping previously treatment-resistant patients. But, like all other antipsychotics before them, these newer drugs do not cure schizophrenia. Nevertheless, it is gratifying to see remarkable improvements in some patients who could not be helped by the first-generation neuroleptics.

Sadly, clozapine use in particular can lead to a very serious side effect—agranulocytosis, which increases susceptibility to infections. This is a life-threatening condition that occurs in about 2% of patients after approximately 1 year of clozapine therapy. It is impossible to know who will develop agranulocytosis and who will not. Fortunately, there is a blood test that tells doctors if a patient is acquiring agranulocytosis. If the patient follows through with frequent blood tests, the deaths caused by this side effect can be prevented. However, the blood tests must be systematic and frequent. Thus, clozapine cannot be used with patients who are too ill to comply with these tests. Other side effects of second-generation antipsychotics include weight gain (except for ziprasidone). First- and second-generation antipsychotic medications are being compared and exhaustively evaluated in several ongoing clinical trials sponsored by the US government (foremost among these is the Clinical Antipsychotic Trials in Intervention Effectiveness, or CATIE) and pharmaceutical companies in the private sector. Quite surprisingly, analyses to date have not shown a clear efficacy advantage of treatment with a second-generation antipsychotic compared to a first-generation neuroleptic. The CATIE in particular has shown that there is some promise in polypharmacy, which is not often a research target but which does seem to lead to greater symptom reductions for more patients than any individual antipsychotic medication.

Other medical treatments

A number of other medications have been suggested for the treatment of schizophrenia. These are too numerous to be discussed in this book. However, patients and families should know that, although neuroleptics are usually the first choice for treatment, other medicines are available for special cases.

For example, lithium has been shown to be effective in some individuals with schizophrenia. For some patients, lithium may be added to neuroleptic treatment to improve its effectiveness. In some cases, drugs called benzodiazapines (often used to treat anxiety) have been helpful. However, they may worsen symptoms in some individuals with schizophrenia. Drugs know as anticonvulsants (because they prevent convulsions in epileptic patients) sometimes work for schizophrenia. This appears to be especially true for violent individuals with schizophrenia and for those who have abnormal brain waves as measured by the electroencephalogram. However, they do not appear to be effective as a maintenance treatment.

Electroconvulsive therapy is known in the popular press as 'electric shock treatment' because it involves the application of an electrical impulse to the patient's brain. Electroconvulsive therapy is useful for some cases of severe depression. However, it has not proved to be helpful for individuals with schizophrenia.

Compliance with medical treatment

Obviously, no medication will be effective if the patient does not take it. Although this is true for all illnesses, it is especially problematic for schizophrenia. The schizophrenic illness makes it difficult—if not impossible—for the patient to understand how important these drugs are. Most people will live with the side effects of drugs that reduce the symptoms of an illness. However, the individual with schizophrenia may not be able to correctly weigh the benefits of treatment against the discomfort of side effects. Also, for some individuals with schizophrenia the drug becomes part of their delusion. They may believe that the doctor is trying to poison them or control their mind for evil reasons.

Due to these problems, nearly half the patients being treated for schizophrenia fail to take their medicine after leaving the hospital. Even when in the hospital, one in five patients does not take the medicine given to them. Failure to take medicine creates a complicated legal, ethical, and medical dilemma. Legally, we cannot force a patient to take medicine or enter a hospital unless the courts determine that the patient is a danger to himself or to others. Ethically, the treatment team ought to provide the best possible treatment. Medically, the best possible treatment is, usually, antipsychotic medication; but patients frequently refuse this alternative.

This dilemma paralyzes clinicians and frustrates family members. Imagine the anguish of parents who, after seeing their child's psychosis clear with drug treatment, must watch his condition worsen because he rejects the medicine. There is no simple solution to this dilemma, but we can take steps to avoid it. Our experience shows that doctors, patients, and their families must deal with this problem during the early phases of treatment. In particular, the doctor and the family must work together to help the patient continue with the treatment. If one member of the family (or perhaps a friend) has earned the patient's trust more than others, that person should play a major role in planning for treatment compliance. Some patients value the advice of a relative or friend much more than that of the doctor.

Of course, friends and family cannot convince the patient to comply with treatment if they do not know why the medicine is so important. Thus, the doctor or other members of the treatment team should spend some time educating them about these issues. We routinely tell families why we believe the medicine works and what types of side effects may occur. When they understand the costs and benefits of treatment they can better convey these to the patient. We also teach friends and family to be good observers of the patient. If we catch the emergence of side effects at an early stage, we can avoid the compliance dilemma by switching the patient to a different drug.

Preparing the patient and family for compliance does not always work. Such cases call for additional action. First, the doctor should determine if the patient is actively refusing medicine or is passively not taking it. This distinction is crucial. For some patients, not taking medicine reflects the negative symptoms of apathy and inactivity. For these patients, not taking medicine is like not leaving the home, not talking with relatives, not dressing themselves, and so on. If this is the case then the doctor can prescribe a long-acting drug.

Most antipsychotic drugs are given in pills. These are short-acting because their effects wear off quickly when the pills are not taken. In contrast, one dose of a long-acting drug can be effective for many weeks. These long-acting antipsychotic drugs have been prepared so that they are absorbed into the body slowly, exerting a therapeutic effect for a relatively long time. However, they are not available in pill form—they must be injected into the body. Since the patient must go to the doctor's office for the injection, this can be inconvenient. Nevertheless, for some patients there is no alternative.

Injectable neuroleptics will not always solve a passive non-compliance problem. Since these long-acting drugs are prepared from a very potent type of neuroleptic, they have more side effects than some neuroleptics taken in pill form. In many cases they are discontinued because the patient begins to actively refuse injections or the doctor determines that the side effects are too severe to justify their use.

If the patient actively refuses medicine, then the doctor should work with the family to learn the reasons for refusal. Many reasons are possible. Some patients are annoyed with side effects but never mention this to their doctor or family. Others have delusions that interfere with treatment. For example, one patient believed that the drug was dissolving his internal organs. We have also known patients who think that they are cured, and that medicine is no longer necessary.

After discovering the reasons for non-compliance, the doctor must establish a plan to try to reverse the patient's decision. In some cases it is possible to reason with the patient. In others, we can achieve compliance by using a different drug. Unfortunately, many refusals of medication cannot be easily reversed. The patient may simply be too ill to realize that treatment is necessary.

When this occurs, a judge in a court of law must determine if the patient is legally a danger to himself or to others. Although there is no simple definition of danger that applies to all patients, several examples should clarify what is meant. Clearly, the patient who plans to hurt or kill another is a danger to society. Some patients may have no clear plan, yet will be considered dangerous if their thoughts or behaviour reveal this to be likely.

The suicidal person presents the most obvious case of a patient dangerous to himself. However, a judge could also reach this conclusion when faced with a non-suicidal patient whose behaviour is likely to lead to injury or death. Some patients refuse to eat; others may place themselves in physical danger. For example, a patient who runs in front of traffic at the command of a hallucination is a danger to himself.

We emphasize that the final determination of dangerousness is a legal, not a medical decision. Although the doctor's opinion will strongly influence a judge's decision, the doctor does not have the authority to treat a non-compliant patient without legal approval. Of course, the authority of the doctor will depend on the legal system where the patient is being treated.

Psychotherapy

Psychological treatment is a very broad term. It refers to any therapeutic approach seeking to modify thoughts and behaviour by talking with patients and/or their families. This does not mean that psychological and medical therapies cannot be used at the same time. In fact, for many individuals with schizophrenia this is the ideal treatment plan. In psychotherapy, patients meet periodically with a therapist to talk about problems that may not be directly related to the causes of schizophrenia. There are many types of psychotherapy and these differ dramatically. Some have patients recall events from childhood; the therapist says very little, but tries to guide patients towards insights about their life and their problems. Other psychotherapies deal only with patients' day-to-day problems; these therapists often help patients solve specific problems (e.g., finding a job).

After examining scientific studies of psychotherapy for schizophrenia and other disorders, the American Psychiatric Association Commission on Psychotherapies concluded that, although useful for many other psychiatric problems, psychotherapy was not an effective treatment for schizophrenia. The Commission did not rule out psychotherapy for individuals with schizophrenia, but it clearly indicated that it should be seen as an addition to drug treatment, not a replacement.

In the treatment of schizophrenia, the skills of the psychotherapist are useful in a variety of ways. The development of a productive patient–therapist relationship will foster compliance with drug therapy and motivation for the behavioural and family treatments we discuss later. By helping the patient deal with the social and psychological consequences of schizophrenia, the psychotherapist can become a valuable ally.

Behavioural therapy

Behavioural therapy is different from other psychological treatments in several ways. Unlike many psychotherapies, its goal is to change what patients do (behaviour) using scientific principles of learning discovered by psychologists. Supported by decades of psychology research, these principles describe the laws that govern learning. Behavioural therapists use these laws to change behaviour in their patients.

One prominent class of behavioural therapies is called cognitive behavioural therapy (CBT). CBT is very effective in a range of psychiatric disorders, but has only more recently been employed in schizophrenia, where it is presently accepted as a complement to medication management. CBT has been shown to help effectively manage positive and negative symptoms, as well as improve patients' adherence to medication regimens and compliance with medical advice. In some cases, CBT may also improve insight, reduce aggression, and even help in the management of positive and negative symptoms in schizophrenia. With regard to negative symptoms, CBT in schizophrenia often focuses on the patient's inability to deal with social situations. One goal is to help the patient achieve an ideal level of social activity. For example, marked social isolation appears to produce more schizophrenic deterioration. On the other hand, too much social activity may produce an increase in psychotic symptoms. If counselors and relatives do not understand the need for the schizophrenic to control social activity and the protective nature of some social withdrawal, they may place too much pressure on the patient to engage in social activities.

The behavioural rehabilitative program for a patient with schizophrenia must be tailored to the particular handicaps of that patient. Many alternatives are available. In what follows, we briefly review three behavioural methods that have been effective in the treatment of schizophrenia: reward and punishment, social skills training, and family therapy.

Reward and punishment

The effects of reward and punishment on behaviour are obvious. We usually do things that are rewarded and avoid activities that are punished. Examples of rewards can be money, products, and social recognition. Punishment can be the withdrawal of a reward or the infliction of physical or emotional harm. Psychology's principles of learning describe how the systematic manipulation of rewards and punishments changes behaviour. These principles have been systematically applied to individuals with schizophrenia in a therapeutic program known as the token economy. The token economy is only useful for treatment settings where patients can be observed for long periods of time. These include hospital wards (where the patient stays overnight), day hospitals (where the patient stays only during the day), and group homes (supervised homes for several patients).

A 'token' is any object that is small and easily identified (e.g., a poker chip). The tokens are used to reward patients for appropriate behaviour. At first, the tokens are given to patients regardless of their behaviour. This is necessary so that the patients can learn that the tokens have value. This learning occurs because they can use tokens to buy rewards from the staff. These rewards are usually valued items (e.g., special foods) or privileges (e.g., access to the television or game rooms).

The patient learns the value of tokens by buying rewards from the staff with the tokens given at the outset of the program. Eventually, the patient must earn tokens. Tokens are earned according to rules specified by staff in an individualized behavioural program. The program specifies the types and degree of behaviour change required to earn a specified number of tokens.

Token economies can teach appropriate self-care and social behaviours to individuals with schizophrenia. Unfortunately it is often difficult for the patient to continue these changes after leaving the program.

Another problem with this method is that, to increase the frequency of a desired behaviours, the patient must be seen doing the behaviours—even if only rarely. For example, we may wish to teach a very ill patient how to converse with others. If he never talks to others a token economy cannot help. If he talks to others rarely, then by rewarding conversation with tokens, we can increase his level of social conversation. In many cases, the patient will not emit the desired behaviour in any form. This is often the case for social behaviours. Indeed, many patients emit very little, if any, appropriate social behaviour. Response acquisition procedures were created to deal with this problem. As the name indicates, these methods help patients acquire a response (that is, a behaviour) that they do not currently do. Since this work has mostly focused on social behaviours, these techniques are often referred to as social skills training.

Social skills training

Social skills training is usually performed with groups of patients. This creates an artificial social situation that is useful for teaching social behaviour.

Although the details of the method vary among hospitals and clinicians, each of these methods shares a common feature: the therapists actively teach the patients how to use verbal and non-verbal behaviour in social situations.

One program, developed by Dr James Curran at Brown University, uses groups of three or four patients and two co-therapists. In a typical therapy session, the therapists complete eight tasks. 1) The therapists review the social behaviours that had been learned in the previous section. They also determine whether the patients practised these behaviours outside of the training session. Clearly, social skills training will be useless if patients do not practise the newly learned behaviour in real social situations. 2) Next, the therapists present a summary of the lesson to be taught during the session. This clarifies what behaviour is to be learned and why it is useful in social situations. 3) Since patients learn best by observation, the therapists perform the skill described in the lesson or present a video tape of someone doing so. The patients observe the performance and are encouraged to ask questions as needed. 4) Since many individuals with schizophrenia are very passive and will not ask questions, the therapists quiz the patients on what they have observed in order to be certain that they were attending to the lesson. 5) Next, it is the patients' turn to practise the newly learned social behaviour. The patients usually practise in pairs, one pair at a time. Their performance is video-taped. 6) The group observes the video-taped behaviour of the patients. The therapist then leads a discussion designed to provide feedback to the patients on tape and to help others learn more about how to practise the skill. 7) After all patients have had an opportunity for feedback, they work in pairs to master the skill with repeated practise. 8) The session ends with the therapists asking the patients to practise the newly learned social skill outside of the therapy session. They usually set a very reasonable goal. For example, they might ask the patients to practise the skill one time each day.

Behavioural family therapy

Although the family environment does not play a role in the *aetiology* or cause of schizophrenia, it may affect the *course* of the illness. In other words, specific types of family interaction may worsen schizophrenic symptoms and result in increased rates of relapse and hospitalization. Thus, behavioural family therapy assumes that family behaviours have an impact on the course of the illness but does not assume that the illness was directly or indirectly caused by deviant family interaction. Its goal is to reduce stress in the patient's life and to encourage the family to participate in the treatment of the illness.

As pioneered by Dr Ian Falloon in Great Britain, there are three major components to behavioural family therapy: education, communication, and problem solving. The educational component tries to reduce the family's self-blame for the illness. When family members blame themselves for their relative's schizophrenia, tensions and bad feelings can create an atmosphere that is, psychologically, not healthy for either patient or the family. Once families learn about the biological bases of the illness, they can throw off guilty feelings and be more helpful in the treatment of their schizophrenic relative. Understanding biological bases also helps families accept the necessity of neuroleptic medication. Some people still see psychiatric medicine as a 'chemical strait-jacket' that does more harm than good. This incorrect belief can be countered by effective education.

Families are also taught that patients cannot control their schizophrenic symptoms. Telling a patient to 'stop being paranoid' or complaining that they are 'too lazy' can be harmful. Patients cannot control their paranoid thoughts or the apathy and withdrawal of the negative symptom syndrome. Accusing the patient of being purposefully symptomatic stresses the patient and frustrates the relative. This clearly leads to a stressful family environment.

We also teach relatives not to communicate high expectations for social or occupational performance to the patient. Many individuals with schizophrenia will never work and never marry. If they do work it is usually in a relatively low-paying, low-prestige job. Families should be pleased to see a schizophrenic relative succeed at even the lowest-paying job—that is a real accomplishment for someone with such a disabling illness. Of course, we do not intend to discourage schizophrenic people from achieving their best. Some patients with milder forms of schizophrenia can achieve much more than the average person with schizophrenia. Our goal here is for both patients and families to honestly assess what a 'reasonable' expectation is.

Perhaps, most importantly, the families are taught how to identify potential stresses for the patient in their home environment. We emphasize that although we can define stress and give examples from the research literature, its definition is often unique to an individual patient. Families must learn to be sensitive to the patient in this regard. By learning how the patient reacts to stress, and by opening up lines of communication, families can lower the stress level and create a healthier environment for the patient.

Of course, opening up lines of communication may not be easy in some families. Many families do not have the communication skills needed to benefit fully from the educational component of treatment. Thus, response acquisition methods are often used to teach these skills. The method of teaching is similar to that described for patients, although it emphasizes those communication skills that are most needed in the family environment. Some families can identify relevant problems but do not have the skills to find and implement solutions. Thus, problem-solving family therapies have been used with some success in reducing schizophrenia relapse rates to a clinically significant degree.

Other considerations

Psychological treatments in conjunction with drug treatment may help prevent schizophrenic relapse. In one study a behavioural treatment included social case work designed to assist the patients in coping with their major roles, in job situations, and vocational rehabilitation counseling. Two years after leaving the hospital, 80% of patients who received neither neuroleptics nor therapy had relapsed. In contrast, only 48% of the patients receiving medicine only had relapsed. Patients who received both therapy and medicine did better than those taking medicine alone; therapy alone reduced the relapse rate of those who had been rehabilitated to the community for 6 months, but after a year it lost its effect except in those patients on active drugs. This study suggested that maximum benefit can be obtained from a combined treatment of medicine and behaviour therapy for at least 1 year after discharge.

It was also found that therapy had improved adjustment and personal relationships in patients with few schizophrenic symptoms since discharge, but had actually hastened relapse in those patients with severe schizophrenic symptoms. On the basis of this finding, the investigators recommended therapy only for those patients currently without schizophrenic symptoms. They suggested that behaviour therapy may be harmful to those with severe and overt symptoms because such patients cannot comprehend the therapy and therefore feel unable to cope with the new challenges it brings.

Indeed, many investigators have confirmed that too-vigorous rehabilitation can result in over-stimulation and relapse of positive schizophrenic symptoms such as delusions and hallucinations. For example, Dr J.K. Wing and colleagues of the British Medical Research Council Social Psychiatry Research Unit reported in 1964 that delusions and hallucinations re-emerged in a group of chronic individuals with schizophrenia who were put directly into an industrial rehabilitation unit. This could have been prevented by adequate preparation of the patients, for example by encouraging them to participate in the work periods on the ward, followed by sessions in the occupational training unit of the hospital.

Other types of therapy, if not done carefully, may over-stimulate the patient and result in the reappearance of positive schizophrenic symptoms. For instance, intense group psychotherapy designed to uncover 'unconscious motivation' and 'role function' may worsen schizophrenic symptoms. Recreational therapy, occupational therapy, group activity, and resocialization therapy may also be potential sources of over-stimulation, if carried out too vigorously.

On the other hand, other work finds a connection between an under-stimulating environment, such as the chronic wards of a large mental hospital, and negative schizophrenic symptoms—apathy, lack of initiative, slowness, social isolation, and poverty of speech. Therefore, in treating schizophrenic patients one walks a tightrope: under-stimulation may lead to negative symptoms on one side and over-stimulation may lead to positive symptoms on the other. Neuroleptics can provide some protection against over-stimulation, but indiscriminate use of the drugs over a long period of time may lead to troublesome neurological complications in some patients. Behavioural therapies may encourage chronic patients to come out from their isolation, but can precipitate the reappearance of positive symptoms. In treating people with schizophrenia one is essentially aiming to provide the optimum conditions for extremely vulnerable people.

Hospitalization

Over the past century, the psychiatric hospital has undergone dramatic changes. Initially, such hospitals were no better than prisons. Patients were physically restrained and, because of lack of medical knowledge, little real treatment was available. Gradually, these warehouses of human turmoil and despair became real hospitals. Patients with schizophrenia received treatment but were rarely helped to a significant degree until neuroleptic medication became available.

For many schizophrenic patients, psychiatric hospitalization is, at times, necessary. Hospitalization is used for four basic reasons: diagnostic evaluation, regulation of medication, reduction of danger to the patient or others, and management of acute problems. Rarely is the hospital used for chronic care as in the past. For most patients, lengthy hospitalization has not been found to be more effective than brief hospitalization.

The longer a patient has been in hospital, the less likely it is that he will want to leave. Lengthy hospital stays can exacerbate negative schizophrenic symptoms and cause an 'institutionalization' syndrome, manifested by loss of interest and initiative, lack of individuality, submissiveness, and deterioration of personal habits. Therefore it is important to minimize the patient's stay in a psychiatric hospital after the initial phase of positive symptoms is under control. Unless there is a special indication that he should stay, the earlier the discharge, the better. Many studies support the benefits of such early discharge. The family life of the patient and his immediate relatives is less disrupted. Today, the trend is towards short hospitalizations with an emphasis on outpatient care.

Of course, this policy of early discharge can be carried too far. It is not advisable to discharge every patient indiscriminately within, say, 2 weeks of admission without proper preparation for his return to the community. The referral of patients to community care without taking into consideration whether there are available facilities has resulted in increased numbers of schizophrenic patients who are homeless or inadequately housed, unemployed, and unable to care for themselves. These unemployed schizophrenic patients in the community spend approximately the same time doing nothing as they did in the chronic wards of mental hospitals. However, unlike the hospitalized patient, the homeless patient in the community is subject to the ravages of crime, poor shelter, and lack of food.

An over-emphasis on community care also puts a strain on the members of the patient's family. The consequence of these burdens on the relatives has been studied: the relatives of nearly 30% of first-admitted and 60% of previously admitted schizophrenic patients had suffered one or more problems which they attributed directly to having to care for the patient. Fortunately, patient and family support groups—like the National Alliance for the Mentally Ill—can help families cope with the burden of caring for a schizophrenic family member.

While the patient is in hospital receiving treatment for positive symptoms, every effort should be made to evaluate his strengths and weaknesses and those of his key relatives or friends. All available community facilities, such as the mental health clinic, day-care center, vocational guidance center, and half-way house, should be assessed. Once the appropriate facility has been selected, liaison with staff there and other preparations should be initiated while the patient is still in hospital. Long-range treatment plans can be established only if such preparations are carefully made. If the patient needs only a short hospital stay, the importance of maintenance drug treatment, particularly after discharge, should be emphasized to both patient and relatives.

Long-term hospital care

Early discharge from hospital may not be possible for some patients. Their positive symptoms may not respond to ordinary doses of neuroleptics, or the side effects may be so severe that constant changes of doses or changes from one type of neuroleptic to another are required. Some patients may need relatively lengthy preparation for discharge because they lack working skills or education. In many cases, patients are poor and may not have the funds needed to resettle in the community. Others may have long-standing negative schizophrenic symptoms with occasional relapses of positive symptoms; even after they have been relieved by antipsychotic drugs, the persistence of negative symptoms will prevent them from early reintegration in the community.

Rehabilitation of chronic patients

Rehabilitation of chronic patients takes time and patience. After the plan and goal have been set up, persistent effort is needed to achieve them. Not only professional skills but also administrative talents are required to carry out the successful rehabilitation of chronic schizophrenic patients. Rehabilitation involves a gradual progression from working on a simple task in the hospital, to more complex tasks in a sheltered workshop outside the hospital, and eventually a return to full employment in the community. We should use all available resources to rehabilitate each patient step-by-step, at his own pace. Compassion, determination, tolerance, and understanding are essential if we are to help these patients and their families.

Those involved with the care of patients with schizophrenia should realize that over-enthusiasm, emotional over-involvement, and disregard for advances in therapeutic methods may be harmful to patients and their families. It is necessary to keep in mind that the exact nature of schizophrenia is still unknown. More research is needed to evaluate the effectiveness of the current treatment programs, some of which are blindly accepted and used in routine day-to-day work. Accordingly, careful clinical observations made with a critical mind and an eye open for problems that might need further research are important at this stage. Interdisciplinary cooperation of all professionals—psychiatrists, general practitioners, psychologists, nurses, social workers, occupational therapists, recreational therapists, and counselors—is vital. Finally, the value of the experience of the patients and their families in coping with schizophrenia should not be underestimated if treatment programs are to be carried out effectively.

We must again emphasize that although scientists have not yet completed a blueprint describing the causes of schizophrenia, we can still help patients and their families to relieve their suffering. We also highlight a crucial point: treatment begins with diagnosis. Although emergency treatment will proceed without a complete diagnosis, an appropriate treatment plan cannot be created without a comprehensive diagnosis. It would be a tragic mistake if the doctor did not learn that street drugs, a brain tumour, or some other problem had caused the schizophrenic symptoms in a patient given the diagnosis of schizophrenia.

Schizoaffective disorder

Advances in the treatment of schizophrenia have thus far benefited patients with severe spectrum disorders, such as schizoaffective disorder, far more than they have patients with 'milder' spectrum disorders, such as schizotypal, schizoid, and paranoid personality disorders, or schizotaxia. As expected based upon its confluence of affective and psychotic features (and the fact that diagnostic inaccuracy may cause schizophrenic and bipolar disordered patients to receive this diagnosis), schizoaffective disorder has been examined most often for clinical responsiveness to both mood-stabilizing and antipsychotic medications. A review of these studies dictates a fairly clear treatment regimen for both bipolar and depressive types of schizoaffective disorder. Historically, either typical antipsychotics or lithium alone were used to manage some cases of the bipolar type of schizoaffective disorder, whereas the co-administration of these two compounds was more effective and, thus, preferable. For the treatment of the depressive type of schizoaffective disorder, combined treatment with antipsychotics and antidepressants was not superior to treatment with antipsychotics alone. However, the efficacy of neither of these treatment strategies was ever evaluated in controlled clinical trials. This is of little consequence, however, as these routines are no longer the preferred strategies for the management of the disorder. In fact, a newer generation of medications has supplanted lithium and typical antipsychotic treatments for many patients.

Newer mood stabilizers such as valproate and carbamazepine, and second-generation antipsychotics such as clozapine and risperidone, have for some individuals greater efficacy and, accordingly, their use is increasing, while the use of valium and typical antipsychotics has diminished. For example, a 1150 mg dose of divalproex can improve Clinical Global Impression Scale scores in 75% of bipolar-type schizoaffective disordered patients, and very few of these patients will suffer serious side effects that would merit discontinuation. A mean dose of 643 mg per day of carbamazepine will lower adherence more than lithium administration, but for those in whom it is well tolerated, carbamazepine reduces hospitalization, recurrence, and concomitant psychotropic medication usage, especially among those with depressive-type schizoaffective disorder.

A regimen of 4.7 mg per day of risperidone has been shown to lower Young Mania Rating Scale scores by 18.0 points after 6 weeks, and Positive and Negative Syndrome Scale by 20 points, Hamilton Rating Scale of Depression scores by 6.6 points, and Clinical Global Impressions scores by 1 point after 4 weeks. Also, when compared to haloperidol, risperidone is better tolerated and provides better symptom relief on at least a subset of clinical scales. For example, risperidone is 14% more effective than haloperidol in reducing scores on the Positive and Negative Syndrome Scale and more than 60% more effective in lowering scores on the Hamilton Rating Scale of Depression, but is less effective on the Clinician-Administered Rating Scale for Mania. It is important to recognize that treatment protocols involving newer mood stabilizers and/or atypical antipsychotics are not effective for some patients, and that their efficacy has been refuted in selected research reports; however, the majority of work on schizoaffective disorder suggests that these newer mood stabilizers and antipsychotics can effectively relieve symptoms alone or in combination for a satisfactory proportion of patients.

At doses of 5–20 mg, olanzapine is significantly more effective than haloperidol in treating both the depressive and bipolar types of the disorder. In relative terms, olanzapine is most effective in treating those who are currently manic or depressed. Furthermore, the drug is tolerated better than haloperidol, with fewer serious side effects, but the likelihood of weight gain is higher with olanzapine. Ziprasidone also has dose-related efficacy on total scores of the Brief

Psychotic Rating Scale and Clinical Global Impression, with optimum effects observed at approximate doses of 160 mg per day. As a group, the atypical antipsychotics may have better efficacy for schizoaffective disorder than even for schizophrenia itself, possibly owing to their greater affinity for serotonin 1A, 1D, and 2 receptors.

Antiepileptic agents, including gabapentin and lamotrigine, may also be useful adjunctive treatments for schizoaffective disorder, and may also be effective when solely administered. Gabapentin can produce symptom relief in as many as 75% of schizoaffective disordered patients at a dose of 1440 mg per day, and may be especially effective in helping treatment-resistant cases, suggesting that wider usage of this compound may be indicated in the future if controlled clinical trials support this high level of effectiveness. Lamotrigine has been found effective in limited trials at dosages as low as 200 mg per day, but has maximal effects on mood stability and paranoid symptoms when administered at 400 mg per day.

Non-pharmacological, biologically oriented therapies have shown limited promise as effective treatments for schizoaffective disorder in the absence of adjunctive pharmacologic management. For example, maintenance electro-convulsive therapy was found to increase survival time of a subgroup of patients with schizoaffective disorder, while bright light therapy and repetitive transcranial magnetic stimulation were each reported to help one patient with schizoaffective disorder in case studies. More empirical work is clearly needed before advocating these procedures for widespread use in the treatment of schizoaffective disorder.

Schizophrenia-spectrum personality disorders

Compared with the literature on treatments for schizophrenia and schizoaffective disorder, there are considerably fewer reports on treatments for schizotypal, schizoid, and paranoid personality disorders. Literature reviewed for the Quality Assurance Project (1990) included 294 papers focusing on the treatment of personality disorders, but only 31 of these studies related to the treatment of schizophrenia-spectrum personality disorders, and a limited number of these reported treatment outcomes in a quantitative manner. Moreover, many studies of pharmacotherapeutic interventions for personality disorders have examined subjects with extensive comorbidity, thus making conclusions regarding the specific personality disorder of interest difficult to interpret (subjects with comorbid schizotypal and borderline personality disorders are perhaps the most frequent among this mixed group of subjects).

Fortunately, while such flawed methods still appear in the scientific litera-ture, overall trends indicate that they are becoming phased out in favour of methodologically sound studies with more 'pure' or 'refined' diagnostic groups. However, while it is currently widely recognized that diagnostic accuracy and precision are critical if these disorders are to become well understood and effectively treatable, such well-designed studies may only be presently underway or recently completed. Thus, as is common, the theoretical resolution to the problem has preceded the scientific data to be gained from such insight, and we are, as yet, left without a large number of useful outcome studies of the schizophrenia-spectrum personality disorders. However, general treatment recommendations are presented below, along with selected examples of outcome studies whenever they are available and informative for the selection of a particular treatment.

Schizotypal personality disorder

Because schizotypal personality disorder is a complex and (probably) etiologically heterogeneous disorder, it is not likely that one treatment approach will be useful for all patients. More likely, different treatments and combinations of therapies will be the most useful for different presentations of schizotypal personality disorder.

Patients with schizotypal personality disorder often view their worlds as odd and threatening places; thus, these individuals may require extended courses of treatment. As with most personality disorders, psychotherapeutic intervention is indicated, while the prospect of pharmacotherapy (other than for acute phases of the illness) largely remains an ambitious goal for the future. Rapport and trust between the clinician and patient may be difficult to establish in schizotypal personality disorder; yet, these elements are crucial for the success of any therapy. This can be facilitated by establishing a warm, client-centered therapeutic environment in which the patient's delusional or inappropriate beliefs are not directly challenged, but instead slowly rationalized.

In light of the frequent occurrence of paranoia and suspiciousness (among other positive symptoms, negative symptoms, and neuropsychological deficits), exploratory psychotherapeutic approaches by themselves are less likely to facilitate positive change than are approaches that emphasize supportive and cognitive behavioural therapies. Such approaches often emphasize concrete interim goals, and stipulate explicit means of attaining them. Because individuals with this disorder are particularly vulnerable to decompensation during times of stress and may experience transient episodes of psychosis, they can also benefit from techniques to facilitate stress reduction (e.g., relaxation techniques, exercise, yoga, and meditation). Fortunately, there is evidence that at least some individuals with schizotypal features are likely to seek treatment in times of stress.

In addition to psychiatric symptoms, other issues should be addressed in therapy, including an understanding of the patient's cognitive strengths and weaknesses. This may help patients confront and cope with long-standing difficulties in their lives. For instance, individuals may present with deficits in attention, verbal memory, or organizational skills that have contributed to failures in a variety of educational, occupational, and social endeavors, and reinforced negative self-images and the experience of performance anxiety. Knowledge of their more circumscribed cognitive capabilities might allow patients to reframe their difficulties in a more benign manner, and also facilitate a more realistic selection of personal, educational, and occupational goals.

To some extent, deficits in specific cognitive domains can also be attenuated. For example, deficits in the acquisition, organization, and retrieval of information may be reduced by standard procedures for these types of difficulties (e.g., writing information down in a 'memory notebook,' use of appointment books, and rehearsal of new information). In addition, social skills training and family therapy may help relieve social anxiety and overcome feelings of isolation from others. Intensive case management and day-hospital admission may also prove helpful—but more costly—treatment approaches.

Although the psychotherapeutic interventions discussed above appear reasonable and appropriate for use in treating schizotypal personality disorder, more research is needed to determine which approaches are most effective. As noted above, there is a paucity of such studies at the present time. It is clear that little therapeutic change is seen following a course of analytic psychotherapy. In one retrospective study, the Global Assessment Scale was measured in patients with several diagnoses upon admission to a psychiatric hospital. One of these groups was diagnosed with DSM-III schizotypal personality disorder, and another group consisted of patients with schizotypal personality disorder and comorbid borderline personality disorder. Patients remained hospitalized for an average of 16.6 months and were followed up an average of 13.6 years after primary treatment consisting of intensive psychoanalytic therapy. Patients admitted with schizotypal personality disorder did demonstrate significant improvement at follow-up; however, after such a long follow-up period, treatment effects are difficult to discern from the effects of other potentially intervening variables, such as life events, or simply the passage of time. In a study of former inpatients given retrospective DSM-III diagnoses of schizotypal personality disorder approximately 15 years after treatment, subjects with pure schizotypal personality disorder showed, at best, only moderate levels of function at follow-up; for example, on a scale of global functioning in which 0 = continuously disabled and 4 = normal, the mean score among patients formerly diagnosable with schizotypal personality disorder was only 1.6.

Marginally beneficial effects of day hospitals on the outcome of schizotypal personality disorder have also been documented. An intensive treatment regimen consisting of psychodynamically oriented individual and group therapy, art therapy, and daily community meetings for an average of 5.5 months produced little change on either the Global Symptom Index or the Health Sickness Rating Scale. At follow-up, there was a moderate decline in symptoms, but global functioning remained poor.

Several studies have investigated the usefulness of medications in treating schizotypal personality disorder, although most investigations employed small numbers of subjects and combined samples of schizotypal and borderline personality disorders. For these reasons, conclusions about the effectiveness of treatment must be conservative. Typical antipsychotics in particular have been proposed to reduce positive symptoms or depressed mood in times of acute stress, but the high incidence of adverse side effects may discourage their widespread use at other times, including the more chronic, stable (i.e., non-crisis) phases of the disorder. Other types of medication have shown generally non-specific effects. For example, fluoxetine is commonly tested for efficacy in schizotypal personality disorder, and it has been shown to reduce scores on several scales of the Hopkins Symptom Checklist, including the total score, the obsessive-compulsive, interpersonal sensitivity, depression, anxiety, and paranoid ideation/psychoticism subscales in a combined group of patients with DSM-IIIR schizotypal and borderline personality disorder; however, in groups consisting solely of patients with schizotypal personality disorder, these reductions were not significant.

Schizoid personality disorder

As with schizotypal personality disorder, the presentation and presumed causes of schizoid personality disorder are believed to be numerous. The heterogeneity of the disorder, its chronic nature, and its characterization by negative symptoms that do not generally foster an optimal therapeutic atmosphere, make this personality disorder particularly difficult to treat. In addition to these limitations, the virtual absence of outcome studies of the disorder complicates the advancement of general treatment recommendations; yet, some agreed-upon treatment options are presented below.

The isolation, anhedonia, and restricted affect of schizoid personality disorder can only be ameliorated under optimal clinical conditions consisting of solid rapport and a stable therapeutic environment in which the patient can learn to rely on the support provided by the clinician, especially during times of crisis. Existing studies have supported the role of CBT in developing social skills and increasing interpersonal sensitivity, while supportive (rather than insightful or interpretive) psychotherapy is generally considered useful. Analytical approaches may not be well tolerated by the patient, and should be relinquished in favour of practical, goal-oriented therapy. Thus, setting concrete and agreed-upon treatment objectives may help enrich and extend the therapeutic experience. To increase interpersonal skills and overall social motivation, group therapy may be indicated, but only for the most high-functioning patients. Pharmacologic intervention in schizoid personality disorder has not been traditionally advocated, except to attenuate anxiety or depression during crises. However, there is hope that this condition will become amenable to psychopharmacologic management in the future. The general recommendations provided above have yet to be tested experimentally for efficacy; rather, they are based on practical guidelines that are in desperate need of fortification by the results of clinical outcome studies.

Paranoid personality disorder

Individuals with paranoid personality disorder rarely present themselves for treatment. It should not be surprising, then, that there has been little outcome research to suggest which types of treatment are most effective with this disorder. Research studies that have examined the effects of various treatments on paranoid symptoms have usually done so within the context of other conditions, such as anxiety disorders or post-traumatic stress disorder; thus, studies of 'pure' paranoid personality disorder are almost non-existent. Generally, family or group therapies are ineffective, and are not recommended. It is likely that, due to the patient's characteristic mistrust, a supportive, client-centered environment will be the optimal setting for therapeutic change. As with the other schizophrenia-spectrum personality disorders, building rapport is difficult, again due to the fundamentally guarded nature of the disorder. Stability in the therapeutic setting is also critical to increase the patient's trust. As with the delusions of schizotypal personality disorder, it is critical that the clinician remain objective and supportive rather than confrontational when entertaining the patient's paranoid ideas. An honest, practical, goal-oriented approach without presenting too much insightful observation or interpretation may work best with paranoid patients.

Pharmacologic treatment and management of paranoid personality disorder is not widely supported, although certain medications can be useful during the more severe bouts of illness. For example, diazepam can be used to reduce severe anxiety, whereas administration of a neuroleptic or atypical antipsychotic may be indicated if decompensation becomes severe. However, these medications should be used sparingly to prevent the emergence of counter-therapeutic effects as a result of the patient's underlying mistrust and fear of being manipulated.

Schizotaxia

There is evidence that the social dysfunction, negative symptoms, and neuropsychological deficits observed in many of the schizotaxic, non-psychotic relatives of individuals with schizophrenia can be ameliorated by various treatment strategies. The negative symptoms of this condition, along with social deficits, can be at least partially treated by some of the same psychotherapeutic and psychosocial methods that are effective in treating schizotypal and schizoid personality disorders. In addition to these methods, psychopharmacologic interventions may be a feasible option in the future.

In one small pilot study, non-psychotic first-degree relatives of patients with schizophrenia who showed moderate levels of negative symptoms and moderate deficits in two or more neuropsychological domains (i.e., attention/working memory, long-term verbal memory, and/or executive functions) were treated with small doses of the novel antipsychotic risperidone. Six subjects who met these criteria were started at 0.25 mg per day, and their dosages were gradually increased to a maximum of 2.0 mg per day for 6 weeks. Negative symptoms declined in five out of six subjects and, in three cases, these improvements were substantial (e.g., total scores on the Scale for Assessment of Negative Symptoms were reduced by about 50%), while effects were more modest in two cases (total scores on the Scale for the Assessment of Negative Symptoms were reduced by about 25%). Five out of six cases also showed substantial improvements (of 1–2 standard deviations) in attention and working memory over the 6-week period. The sixth subject, who had lower overall cognitive abilities, did not demonstrate improvement in clinical or cognitive measures. In addition, side effects were temporary and mainly mild. Replication of these effects in a large, controlled sample could prove revolutionary not only for the treatment of clinically impaired (but non-psychotic) relatives of individuals with schizophrenia, but also for early intervention and primary prevention of schizophrenia.

Our understanding of the pathology of schizophrenia and its treatment has advanced greatly over the last century, and exponential gains have been made in the last four decades. This knowledge has had tangible impacts on the disease: inpatient admissions and their length of stay in psychiatric hospitals have steadily decreased, and more patients are managing their disease effectively, especially through the use of psychotropic medication. These advances have also benefitted our understanding of other schizophrenia-spectrum disorders, especially the more severe conditions such as schizoaffective disorder and schizotypal personality disorder.

11

What courses and outcomes are possible in schizophrenia?

> ## → Key points
>
> ◆ Studies of course and outcome support Kraepelin's original conclusions: the course and outcome of schizophrenia are, on the average, worse than those of mood disorders.
>
> ◆ However, some patients with schizophrenia can recover from the illness or experience a relatively benign outcome.
>
> ◆ The course and outcome of schizophrenia can be modified by environmental factors, such as stress and the family environment.

Kraepelin described one of the core features of schizophrenia to be its progressively deteriorating course with little chance of recovery. In contrast, mood disorders were thought to have an episodic course with good intermorbid functioning and a relatively benign outcome. The ensuing decades of research have painted a more complex picture of the course and outcome of schizophrenia. Most notably, in contrast to Kraeplin's bleak outlook, more than a trivial number of patients can more or less successfully recover from schizophrenia. Dr Manfred Bleuler, son of Dr Eugen Bleuler, reported a 20-year follow-up of over 200 individuals with schizophrenia excluding those who had either died or shown little psychiatric stability over the previous 5 years. Bleuler noted that one in five patients had recovered to normal levels of social functioning and were free of psychotic symptoms. Furthermore, one in three patients manifested a relatively benign outcome. Thus, while patients still experienced hallucinations and delusions, they exhibited only mild impairments in social functioning and very few outward behavioural problems. These results are especially remarkable given that the study was completed prior to the discovery of antipsychotic medications.

Dr Luc Ciompi was able to follow nearly 300 patients for as long as 50 years after hospitalization. Using Bleuler's categories of outcome, Ciompi found 27% of the patients to be fully recovered, 22% to have mild symptoms, 24% to have moderately severe symptoms, and 18% to have severe symptoms. Nine per cent of the sample had an uncertain outcome. A progressively deteriorating, insidious onset was observed in 49% of the patients, while a sudden or acute onset of illness with little or no difficulties in premorbid functioning was reported for the rest of the sample. Forty-eight per cent of the patients had a continuous course of illness and the remainder had an episodic course. In addition, an episodic course was more likely among patients with acute onset. Acute onset and episodic course were both associated with better long-term outcome.

A study performed by Dr Ming Tsuang and colleagues, known as the Iowa 500 study, followed 186 individuals with schizophrenia, 86 manics, and 212 depressives for 35–40 years. As a general index of social competence, the proportion of each group that eventually married was recorded, and was found to vary markedly between the groups. For example, while only 21% of individuals with schizophrenia married during the follow-up period, 70% of manics, 81% of depressives, and 89% of surgical control subjects had done the same. The ability to function outside of an institutional setting was seen in 34% of the individuals with schizophrenia, 69% of the manics, 70% of the depressives, and 90% of the controls. In close approximation of these findings, productive occupational functioning characterized 35% of the individuals with schizophrenia, 67% of the manics, 67% of the depressives, and 88% of the controls. Also, the percentage of each group with no psychiatric symptoms at follow-up was 20% for individuals with schizophrenia, which is the same proportion noted by Bleuler. However, this figure does not compare favourably with the symptom-free outcomes of 50% for manics, 61% for depressives, and 85% for controls.

The World Health Organization followed the course of over 1000 psychotic patients for over 2 years. That study found no relationship between diagnostic category and the length of the psychotic episode leading to ascertainment; however, the average length of psychotic episode tended to be longer in schizophrenia. Furthermore, psychosis was more prevalent at follow-up in the schizophrenic sample (37%) than in either the manic or the depressive samples (26 and 14%, respectively), and individuals with schizophrenia were psychotic for a greater percentage of the 2-year follow-up period than the affective patients were. In sum, the course of illness was more severe for the individuals with schizophrenia.

Overall, studies of course and outcome support Kraepelin's original conclusions: the course and outcome of schizophrenia are, on average, worse than those of mood disorders. However, as these detailed follow-up studies demonstrated, a significant number of patients with schizophrenia can recover or experience a relatively benign outcome. In fact, favourable outcome may be more common among individuals with schizophrenia than was previously believed. At this time, our understanding of factors that mediate the course of schizophrenia is limited, but some progress has been made. From analyses of the World Health Organization outcome data, it seems that levels of work functioning and social relationships prior to the onset of schizophrenia are significant predictors of outcome after the onset of the disorder. In addition, it has been shown that the presence of mood disorder symptoms during a schizophrenic decompensation is a favourable prognostic sign. This connection was noted by Dr George Vaillant, who deduced an association between symptoms of depression and recovery from schizophrenia from a review of 13 prior studies. He found that 80% of 30 recovered individuals with schizophrenia and 33% of 30 non-recovered individuals with schizophrenia had manifested depressive symptoms. Vaillant also demonstrated a strong correlation between depressive symptoms and remission of schizophrenia in a 15-year follow-up study. Several studies have found similar results.

Clarifying the contribution of depressive symptoms to the outcome of schizophrenia may be clinically useful because depression is common in the course of schizophrenia. Over a 6- to 12-year span, it has been reported that 57% of individuals with schizophrenia had one or more depressive episode. These depressed patients with schizophrenia had an otherwise typical course of schizophrenic symptoms. Further, their illness did not appear to begin with depressive symptoms and was not episodic. Early studies also indicated that obsessive or compulsive features might be associated with a more benign course in schizophrenia, but more recent work has suggested just the opposite. This is a crucial distinction to be made, since 14–47% of inpatients with schizophrenia may have such features. Preliminary data suggested that the addition of a serotonin reuptake-blocking medication to typical neuroleptic drugs may be helpful for psychotic patients with obsessive/compulsive features. Further studies are needed to determine whether the presence of such obsessive/compulsive features identifies a true subtype of schizophrenia, and to explore optimal treatment options.

Whatever knowledge has been gained thus far in describing and predicting the course of schizophrenia is due to the high diagnostic stability of schizophrenia as a disorder. The Iowa 500 study demonstrated this fact through a re-evaluation of individuals with schizophrenia over a 35- to 40-year period, in which it was determined that 93% of schizophrenia diagnoses were confirmed. Only 4% of patients originally diagnosed with schizophrenia received a diagnosis of a mood disorder at follow-up. Similarly, others have found high diagnostic stability in a prospective follow-up of 19 narrowly defined individuals with schizophrenia, in which no patients were re-diagnosed with a mood disorder.

Mortality in patients with schizophrenia is elevated compared with the general population, and much of this increase in mortality is due to suicide. As noted earlier, the second-generation antipsychotic clozapine may lessen the suicide risk in such patients.

Although psychosocial factors have not been convincingly shown to influence the aetiology of schizophrenia, these factors can influence the course of the disorder. Much of this research has focused on the role of stressful life events. Although some controversy exists over the best definition for a stressful event, most researchers agree that stressful events are those life circumstances that require physical or psychological adaptation on the part of the patient. Life events may be negative, as in the death of a spouse, or positive, as in the birth of a child. There is no support for the hypothesis that stressful life events predict the onset of schizophrenia. Patients with schizophrenia who relapse, however, tend to have more stressful life events than those who do not relapse, although relapse can occur in the absence of such events and remission can be maintained in their presence. More stressful life events are found for relapsing individuals with schizophrenia taking neuroleptic medication than for relapsing individuals with schizophrenia who are drug-free. This suggests that the protective effects of neuroleptics and the absence of stressful life events may be additive. That is, the availability of one protective factor may compensate for the lack of the other. It is important for patients and doctors to understand these research studies because they provide clues about how to deal with a relative or patient who has schizophrenia. For example, some parents of schizophrenic patients think that it is a good idea to put some pressure on their children to motivate them to work harder, make friendships, or reach other goals. But the life stress research shows that this will be counterproductive. More pressure and stress make the illness worse, not better.

Another productive area of research into the psychosocial moderators of schizophrenia course and outcome focuses on the effects of the patient's family environment. Expressed emotion (EE) describes the emotional reactivity of family members in their interactions with a schizophrenic patient. We measure EE by observing the degree to which family members criticize the patient, express hostility towards the patient, and are emotionally over-involved with the patient. Drs Vaughn and Leff examined EE as a moderator of the 9-month relapse rates in 128 individuals with schizophrenia living with their families and found that 51% of patients in high-EE families relapsed, while only 13% of individuals with schizophrenia in low-EE families did. Furthermore, among individuals with schizophrenia in high-EE families, the risk for relapse was strongly correlated with the amount of time the patient spent in direct contact with the family. In addition, the prophylactic effect of neuroleptic medication differed for patients returning to low-EE and high-EE families. Among the low-EE group, relapse was unrelated to medication status. In high-EE families, however, the relapse rate for unmedicated individuals with schizophrenia was significantly elevated. This increase in recurrence risk was also associated with increased exposure to other members of the family. Remarkably, 92% of unmedicated individuals with schizophrenia in prolonged contact with high-EE families relapsed, but neuroleptic medication reduced this rate to 53%. Most aspects of Vaughn and Leff's study of a British sample were replicated in a 9-month study of individuals with schizophrenia from California. Notably, the Californian study agreed with the British study in finding that a combination of low family contact and regular medication mitigated the effects of having a high-EE family. The Californian study, however, found no medication effect for patients having more than 35 hours of contact per week with high-EE families. Subsequent studies designed to reduce EE in families of individuals with schizophrenia have demonstrated reduced relapse rates due to this intervention.

12

How can affected individuals and their families cope with schizophrenia?

> **⮞ Key points**
>
> ◆ Patients should be under continuous supervision by their psychiatrist during drug therapy, and should only alter that therapy when advised by their psychiatrist.
>
> ◆ Patients and families can help prevent relapse by avoiding stressful situations or parental over-involvement.

How patients can help themselves

Patients learn to cope with schizophrenic symptoms by trial and error. When they have a worsening of symptoms they may learn to seek psychiatric admission rather than resist it. Gradually they learn that discontinuation or decrease of medication leads to a relapse of positive symptoms. They may be able to adjust the dose of drugs to avoid severe side effects, yet maintain a sufficient level to prevent the reappearance of symptoms.

Clearly, not all patients can do this. Nearly half of the out-patients treated for schizophrenia fail to take their medication; the relapse rate is high among such patients. Patients should be under continuous supervision by their psychiatrist during drug therapy. Even if they discover how to adjust the drug dose, they should share and discuss these experiences with their psychiatrist and not attempt to make changes on their own.

If the patient finds it difficult to remember to take tablets, long-acting neuroleptic injections are available; one injection works for an average of 2 weeks. Patients should faithfully follow their doctor's prescription and receive the injection regularly; with time this can be adjusted as needed.

The family has an important role to play in reminding patients to take medicine regularly or to visit the doctor for neuroleptic injections. This is particularly true if they become reluctant to follow doctor's orders and relapse seems imminent. In these cases the family's insistence on taking medication may prevent a full relapse of positive symptoms.

Some patients learn to avoid situations that may precipitate delusions or hallucinations. Examples of these include: heated discussions of politics or religious experiences, indulging in fantasy daydreams, too-frequent contact with family members, and exposure to crowded places. If these situations cannot be avoided, patients can increase the dose of medication to prevent the symptoms from recurring. Most patients are alarmed when they first experience hearing voices, but gradually learn to live with them; they may occur occasionally even during medication. Patients may either ignore the voices or learn not to be upset by them. In some cases the patient hears the voices only when alone and unoccupied. These patients should occupy themselves with routine housework, playing a musical instrument, or concentrating on reading an interesting book, especially if the voices cause distress.

Some patients are able to work and many family members encourage patients to seek gainful employment. Before doing so the family should consult with the doctor to determine if this is a reasonable goal for the patient. The work that patients choose should be well within their competence. An established 'clubhouse', where affected individuals are treated as contributing 'members,' can help in this regard, and give the affected individual a sense of purpose and belonging. They should avoid occupations that are challenging or stressing. Undemanding occupations are particularly therapeutic for chronic schizophrenic patients because they prevent the development and deterioration of negative symptoms such as apathy, withdrawal, and lack of willpower. Of course, family members must learn what is and what is not stressful for the patient. What seems simple and even relaxing to a family member might be quite challenging and stressful for the schizophrenic patient.

Furthermore, too much stimulation or intrusion from relatives, friends, or professionals may trigger schizophrenic symptoms. Some patients know when it is time to withdraw from an over-stimulating environment in order to prevent recurrence. Families must respect the patient's need to be alone. However, excessive social withdrawal may cause negative symptoms to develop. Some intelligent patients can learn from experience to avoid over- and/or under-stimulation and tread the narrow path of ideal conditions.

The role of the patient's family

Most individuals with schizophrenia are unable, without some help from others, to select the ideal conditions to avoid over- and/or under-stimulation. By living with schizophrenia, many families gradually learn how best to help their schizophrenic relatives. It is usually advisable for the patient and his relatives to live together again after the initial episode of positive symptoms is over, but this requires a great deal of patience, understanding, compassion, and sacrifice from the relatives.

The patient's first episode of psychotic symptoms often leaves relatives with alternating feelings of shock, hope, and disappointment. The relatives gradually come to realize that schizophrenia is not a short-term problem: it is a lifelong disorder that requires long-term care. When patients are actively psychotic, they cannot make rational judgements. Their relatives may have to take action on their behalf, such as initiating legal procedures to commit them to hospital. This may be necessary to prevent them from harming themselves or others. Even some time after the initial phase, patients may be unable to comprehend their relatives' actions.

Living with a schizophrenic person can be very stressful. Relatives may find that their continuous efforts to care for the patient require the sacrifice of their own social lives. This can become too much to bear when they obtain from the patient, not appreciation, but resentment. The patient's unpredictable behaviour, such as violence, bizarre behaviour, talking to himself, silly laughter, and giggling (particularly in front of other people), embarrasses others. Some relatives cope with this by firmly telling the patient that this sort of behaviour is allowed only in private. They also discover there is little point in arguing with the patient when he is reciting his delusions or hallucinations.

At times individuals with schizophrenia need to isolate themselves to 'recharge their batteries' before resuming social interaction. At such times it is not helpful if relatives try to cajole the patient out of this solitude. Continuous withdrawal and daydreaming, on the other hand, may accelerate the development of inertia and apathy. Through experience, those who live with schizophrenic people learn when they should be interrupted and drawn out of their self-imposed isolation.

Some parents feel they are to blame for the patient's schizophrenia, and insensitive remarks made by friends or professional people can make matters worse. These feelings of guilt, combined with physical and mental exhaustion in the course of their long-standing emotional burden, can cause real suffering. At this point, parents need to talk and ventilate their feelings to friends and professional people such as social workers, public health nurses, general practitioners, clinical psychologists, and psychiatrists. Sympathetic emotional support may help to alleviate tensions, anxiety, guilt, and unhappiness. Unrealistically high expectations on the part of the relatives may lead to disappointment, frustration, and resentment. It is important for relatives to come to terms with the lifelong nature of the schizophrenic handicap and to realize that some patients may never return fully to their previous selves, in spite of continuous medication, psychosocial therapies, and strenuous rehabilitation efforts. Only when the relatives have accepted a realistic assessment of the patient's condition can realistic goals be set for rehabilitation.

Relatives of individuals with schizophrenia can share their feelings and experiences with others who have similar experiences. By learning from each other and ventilating their feelings of frustration, they can encourage each other to fight the mental incapacity due to schizophrenia. Through participation in such groups, they may also learn what help is available to them in the community, which professionals are most sympathetic and helpful, and how to help the patients and themselves cope effectively with schizophrenia.

When is professional help needed?

Matters concerning medication should be discussed with the patient's psychiatrist, rather than with non-professional people who may recommend new methods of treatment that have not been scientifically evaluated. Neither should family members discontinue drug treatment through fear that their schizophrenic relative will become addicted. No evidence exists for addiction to these drugs and, as emphasized in this book, the drug treatments for schizophrenia help prevent further relapses.

Professional help is also needed if ever the patient talks about committing suicide. The patient then needs immediate attention because the risk of suicide among schizophrenic patients is high; any indication of attempted suicide requires emergency care. The close relatives of patients may also occasionally feel that life is not worth living. Such pessimistic feelings may affect the capacity to cope with daily routines and work, or produce physical symptoms such as loss of weight, sleeplessness, loss of appetite, gastrointestinal upset, and dizziness. Thus, relatives with suicidal thoughts should seek immediate professional attention. It is not easy to be a caregiver for a schizophrenic patient.

At times, caregivers need their own therapy to help them cope with their schizophrenic relative.

In this chapter, we have discussed some of the ways in which patients and families can help themselves. We could have mentioned only the positive aspects, but felt compelled to discuss difficulties that are likely to arise in order to encourage a realistic approach to schizophrenic handicaps. The accumulation of knowledge about schizophrenia is making such an approach increasingly possible. With tolerance and understanding, many patients and families successfully cope with living with schizophrenia. As long as patients, with the support of sympathetic and understanding individuals, can find the narrow path between over- and under-stimulation, they can successfully avoid recurrence of positive or negative symptoms.

Appendix 1

List of family and patient support groups

United Kingdom

MIND (National Association for Mental Health)
15–19 Broadway
Stratford
London E15 4BQ
Tel: 020 8519 2122
Web: www.mind.org.uk

Mental Health Foundation
9th Floor, Sea Containers House
20 Upper Ground
London SE1 9QB
Tel: 020 7803 1100
Web: www.mentalhealth.org.uk

Rethink
89 Albert Embankment
London SE1 7TP
Tel: 0845 456 0455
Web: www.rethink.org

Making Space
Lyne House
46 Allen Street
Cheshire
Warrington WA2 7JB
Tel: 01925 571 680
Web: www.makingspace.co.uk

SANE
1st Floor Cityside House
40 Adler Street
London E1 1EE
Tel: 020 375 1002
Web: www.sane.org.uk
SANELINE: 0845 767 8000 (telephone helpline open 2pm–midnight every day of the year to give information and support)

United States

National Alliance for the Mentally Ill (NAMI)
3803 N. Fairfax Dr., Ste. 100
Arlington
Virginia 22203-3754
Tel: 703 524 7600
Web: www.nami.org

National Mental Health Association
2000 N. Beauregard Street
Alexandria
Virginia 22314-2971
Tel: 703 684 7722
Web: www.nmha.org

The National Alliance for Research on Schizophrenia and Depression
60 Cutter Mill Road
Suite 404
Great Neck
New York 11021
Tel: 516 829 0091
Web: www.narsad.org

Australia

SANE
P.O. Box 226
South Melbourne
Victoria 3205
Tel: (006) 03 9482 4387
Web: www.sane.org

Canada

Schizophrenia Society of Canada
100-4 Fort Street
Winnipeg
MB R3C1C4
Tel: 204 786 1616
Web: www.schizophrenia.ca

Appendix 2

Accessing clinical trials and research studies

CenterWatch

The global source for clinical trials information: offering news, analysis, study grants, career opportunities, and trial listings to professionals and patients.

Contact information:

Mail: CenterWatch
100 N. Washington St., Ste 301
Boston, MA 02114
E-mail: customerservice@centerwatch.com
Tel: (617) 948-5100
Toll-Free: (866) 219-3440
Web: www.centerwatch.com

ClinicalTrialNetwork.com

ClinicalTrialNetwork.com provides a searchable database of clinical investigators to sponsor companies, CROs, and individuals looking to participate in clinical trials.

Contact information:

Mail: Clinical Trial Network, LLC
542 Berlin Cross Keys Road
Unit 3 # 285
Sicklerville, NJ 08081
Tel: (856) 513-0424
E-mail: info@clinicaltrialnetwork.com
Web: www.clinicaltrialnetwork.com

ClinicalTrials.gov

ClinicalTrials.gov is a registry of federally and privately supported clinical trials conducted in the United States and around the world. ClinicalTrials.gov gives you information about a trial's purpose, who may participate, locations, and phone numbers for more details. This information should be used in conjunction with advice from health care professionals.

Contact information:

Web: www.clinicaltrials.gov

Schizophrenia Trials Network

The Schizophrenia Trials Network (STN) has been established to support the conduct of treatment trials on schizophrenia treatment effectiveness in a community setting.

Contact information:

Mail: Ingrid Rojas, STN Program Director
The University of North Carolina at Chapel Hill
Tel: (919) 843-7365
E-mail: irojas@med.unc.edu
Web: www.stn.unc.edu

Further reading

American Psychiatric Association (2000) *Diagnostic and Statistical Manual of Mental Disorders,* 4th edn, Text Revision. Washington, DC: American Psychiatric Publishing.

Faraone SV, Tsuang D, Tsuang MT (1999) *Genetics of Mental Disorders: A Guide for Students, Clinicians, and Researchers.* New York, NY: Guilford Press.

Mueser KT, Gingerich S (2006) *The Complete Family Guide to Schizophrenia: Helping Your Loved One Get the Most Out of Life.* New York, NY: Guilford Press.

Mueser KT, Jeste DV (2008) *Clinical Handbook of Schizophrenia.* New York, NY: Guilford Press.

Saks ER (2007) *The Center Cannot Hold.* New York, NY: Hyperion.

Torrey EF (2006) *Surviving Schizophrenia: A Manual for Families, Patients, and Survivors.* New York, NY: Harper-Collins.

Tsuang MT, Stone WS, Lyons, MJ (2007) *Recognition and Prevention of Major Mental and Substance Use Disorders.* Washington, DC: American Psychiatric Publishing.

Index